See It

Be It

Write It

Using Performing Arts to Improve Writing Skills and Test Scores

Hope Sara Blecher-Sass, Ed.D.
Maryellen Moffitt

free spirit
PUBLISHING®

Library of Congress Cataloging-in-Publication Data
Blecher-Sass, Hope Sara.
  See it, be it, write it : using performing arts to improve writing skills and test scores / Hope Sara Blecher-Sass and Maryellen Moffitt.
       p. cm.
  Includes bibliographical references and index.
  ISBN 978-1-57542-347-0
  1. English language—Study and teaching—United States. 2. Performing arts—Study and teaching—United States. 3. Educational tests and measurements—United States. I. Moffitt, Maryellen. II. Title.
  LB1631.B65 2010
  428.0071—dc22
                                                                        2010000345

At the time of this book's publication, all facts and figures cited are the most current available. All telephone numbers, addresses, and Web site URLs are accurate and active; all publications, organizations, Web sites, and other resources exist as described in this book; and all have been verified as of December 2009. The authors and Free Spirit Publishing make no warranty or guarantee concerning the information and materials given out by organizations or content found at Web sites, and we are not responsible for any changes that occur after this book's publication. If you find an error or believe that a resource listed here is not as described, please contact Free Spirit Publishing. Parents, teachers, and other adults: We strongly urge you to monitor children's use of the Internet.

Some of the information about differentiated instruction in Part 2, pages 54–61, is based on material in *Teaching Beyond the Test: Differentiated Project-Based Learning in a Standards-Based Age* by Phil Schlemmer, M.Ed., and Dori Schlemmer (Minneapolis: Free Spirit Publishing, 2008) and is adapted with permission of the publisher.

Edited by Eric Braun
Cover and interior design by Michelle Lee
Illustrations by Paul Agner
Computer photo © istockphoto.com/YinYang; pencil © istockphoto.com/NickS; faces graphic © istockphoto.com/bubaone

10 9 8 7 6 5 4 3 2 1
Printed in the United States of America

Free Spirit Publishing Inc.
217 Fifth Avenue North, Suite 200
Minneapolis, MN 55401-1299
(612) 338-2068
help4kids@freespirit.com
www.freespirit.com

Dedication

We dedicate this book to Ann Moffitt, Joseph Moffitt, and Louis Blecher, who began this process with us but who passed away before its completion. May this book be a tribute to our never-ending love for them and the memories we will hold in our hearts forever.

Acknowledgments

Thank you to Donna Vaupel for bringing us together in a classroom in Elizabeth, New Jersey.

A Round of Applause to Barbara Tedesco for reintroducing us at breakfast that cold morning in late December.

Thank you to Elizabeth "BJ" Franks for supporting us every step of the way.

A Round of Applause to Loren Ivy Sass whose performance at Union County Dance Centre was our Aha moment. Break a leg!

Thank you to Colin "C.J." Sass and Andrew J. Kuphal for sharing ideas and helping us fine tune the strategies in this book.

We owe a **Round of Applause** to Colin, Lori Krivda, and Alan Blecher, who toasted us as we began in Minneapolis and who saw us through to the end.

Thank you to Dr. Natalie Brown for believing from the very beginning and for building the foundation upon which this book was written.

We owe a **Round of Applause** to our brothers, Robert and Patrick Moffitt, and Alan and Todd Blecher, who have stepped into our dads' empty shoes to provide the encouragement and support we needed then, now, and always.

Thank you to Helen Dorothy Gilman Blecher, who doesn't use a computer but who nevertheless has faith in our abilities.

A Round of Applause to Maggie Moffitt and Kelly Moffitt, who are family but just as much friends and to Carol Ann Giardelli and Sonia Shaub, who are friends but just as much family.

Thank you to those who kept the fire going and checked up on us to make sure we were okay; the great espresso and support in North Plainfield was a tremendous boost.

A Round of Applause to Timothy Peters for patiently responding to our emails and calls. We won't clog your inbox anymore.

Thank you to Raymond Sass for sharing space in the house for papers and props.

A Round of Applause to Marla Zirin and Jackie and Jerry Baranoff for literally answering our call.

Thank you to Abbe Fried, our personal embroidery expert, and Tammy Scott and John DeLaurentis, our personal poets, for adding just the right touches.

A Round of Applause to Rachel Dias, Shayla Edwards, and Moises Philippsborn for being our actors and to the Bergenfield Bunch (Lutz, Kreger, Iozia, Croney, and Jack and Judy S.) for your astounding patience.

Thank you to the administrators, teachers, students and parents who participated in our professional development workshops, presentations, and demonstration lessons, and let us perfect our craft.

A Round of Applause to Judy, John, Marjorie, Eric, Steven, Michelle, and the staff at Free Spirit Publishing in Minnesota for providing us with the ways and means to bring this book to you.

And finally, a **Standing Ovation** to you for reading this book and choosing to use our process.

Contents

List of Reproducible Pages...v

Preface...vii

Introduction...1

Part 1: Using Performing Arts to Improve Writing Skills and Test Scores..5

1. Standards, Assessments, and Getting to Know Your Students 6
2. The Prompt Enactment Process...17
3. The Standing Ovation Checklists...27
4. Encore Performances: Adjusting the Process Throughout the Year 38

Part 2: Extending and Optimizing the Process..53

5. Differentiating the Enactment Process...54
6. Turning Your Classroom Into a Theater..62
7. Social-Emotional Learning and the Enactment Process 68

Part 3: The Types of Writing Prompts...77

8. The Picture Prompt...78
9. The Speculative Prompt 83
10. The Persuasive Prompt..88
11. The Poetry Prompt..97
12. The Quote or Adage Prompt...104
13. Cross-Curricular Connections..110

Part 4: Ready-to-Use Prompts..117

Picture Prompts...118
Speculative Prompts...128
Persuasive Prompts..138
Poetry Prompts..148
Quote and Adage Prompts 158
Themed Prompt Sets...168

References and Resources...178

Index..180

About the Authors 183

List of Reproducible Pages

Writing Assessment Information Fact Sheet 12

Previous Writing Test Data Collection Sheet 13

Assessment Writing Clusters 14

Student Progressive Writing Chart 15

Class Progressive Writing Chart 16

Standing Ovation Checklist Playing Cards (for Picture and Speculative Prompts) 47

Standing Ovation Checklist Playing Cards (for Persuasive Prompts) 49

Standing Ovation Checklist Playing Cards (for Poetry and Quote or Adage Prompts) 51

What's Happening Cards 74

How You Feel About It Cards 75

What You Are Doing Cards 76

Standing Ovation Checklist for Picture Prompts 82

Standing Ovation Checklist for Speculative Prompts 87

Standing Ovation Checklist for Persuasive Prompts 93

Standing Ovation Checklist for Poetry Prompts 101

Standing Ovation Checklist for Quote or Adage Prompts 109

What's in the Box? (Picture Prompt) 118

What's in the Box? (Teacher's Guide) 119

We're in This Together (Picture Prompt) 120

We're in This Together (Teacher's Guide) 121

Ready to Ride (Picture Prompt) 122

Ready to Ride (Teacher's Guide) 123

On My Way (Picture Prompt) 124

On My Way (Teacher's Guide) 125

What's So Funny? (Picture Prompt) 126

What's So Funny? (Teacher's Guide) 127

The Surprise Outside (Speculative Prompt) 128

The Surprise Outside (Teacher's Guide) 129

School Closed (Speculative Prompt) 130

School Closed (Teacher's Guide) 131

A Friend in Need (Speculative Prompt) 132

A Friend in Need (Teacher's Guide) 133

Me? A Winner? (Speculative Prompt) 134

Me? A Winner? (Teacher's Guide) 135

The Class Pet (Speculative Prompt) 136

The Class Pet (Teacher's Guide) 137

Selling a Cell Phone (Persuasive Prompt) 138

Selling a Cell Phone (Teacher's Guide) 139

Message in a Bottle (Persuasive Prompt) 140

Message in a Bottle (Teacher's Guide) 141

Energy Saving Schedule (Persuasive Prompt) 142

Energy Saving Schedule (Teacher's Guide) 143

School Improvement Is Up to You (Persuasive Prompt) 144

School Improvement Is Up to You (Teacher's Guide) 145

Concerned About Curfews (Persuasive Prompt) 146

Concerned About Curfews (Teacher's Guide) 147

Being Part of a Family (Poetry Prompt) 148

Being Part of a Family (Teacher's Guide) 149

Cool Things You Learn in School (Poetry Prompt) 150

Cool Things You Learn in School (Teacher's Guide) 151

A Birthday Superpower Surprise (Poetry Prompt) 152

A Birthday Superpower Surprise (Teacher's Guide) 153

A Favorite Memory (Poetry Prompt) 154

A Favorite Memory (Teacher's Guide) 155

All My Hard Work . . . Ruined! (Poetry Prompt) 156

All My Hard Work . . . Ruined! (Teacher's Guide) 157

Self Determination (Quote or Adage Prompt) 158

Self Determination (Teacher's Guide) 159

Peer Pressure (Quote or Adage Prompt) 160

Peer Pressure (Teacher's Guide) 161

Pride (Quote or Adage Prompt) 162

Pride (Teacher's Guide) 163

Believe in Yourself (Quote or Adage Prompt) 164

Believe in Yourself (Teacher's Guide) 165

Taking a Risk (Quote or Adage Prompt) 166

Taking a Risk (Teacher's Guide) 167

Baseball (Themed Prompt Set) 168

Baseball (Picture Prompt) 169

Lemonade (Themed Prompt Set) 170

Lemonade (Picture Prompt) 171

Recycling (Themed Prompt Set) 172

Recycling (Picture Prompt) 173

Shoes (Themed Prompt Set) 174

Shoes (Picture Prompt) 175

Hard-Knock Life (Themed Prompt Set) 176

Hard-Knock Life (Picture Prompt) 177

Preface

We began teaching writing long before the demands of the No Child Left Behind Act (NCLB) came into play, and we have been teaching it every year since. Writing strategies, mandates, and language arts literacy assessments continue to change at warp speed. Prior to high-stakes testing, educators would celebrate writers who thought "outside the box," but today that kind of thinking can be costly.

This became clear when a precocious third-grade student (we'll call him Henry) happily handed in his state assessment booklet and proudly announced that, since he "didn't like the picture in there," he just made up a story about a dog he saw on his way to school that morning. He assured us it was the best story he had ever written.

Had this incident happened prior to NCLB, we would have smiled and told Henry we looked forward to reading his story. But it didn't, so instead, we tried to conceal the panic we were feeling and asked Henry why he didn't write about the picture in the test booklet. His response was simple.

"I'd rather write about something real," he said.

"Didn't you think the person in the picture prompt was real?" we asked, a little confused.

And to that he replied: "Oh, you mean the person in the picture was supposed to be real? I don't know anyone like that. I'd rather write about a dog."

While Henry's story was certainly unique, his situation wasn't. In fact, a number of our skilled writers scored below the proficient benchmark score on our state's assessment. The low scores left us puzzled and frustrated. Eventually, after many hours spent preparing students for assessments, it became clear that the fault lay with us, not with them. We had left out a step in the writing process. Many students never made a direct connection between the writing prompt and their written response. We assumed our students were able to make this connection automatically. We were wrong.

As teachers, we know students might find it difficult to respond to writing prompts for many reasons. Some ELLs (English language learners) lack the vocabulary and background knowledge to craft a high-scoring response. Some prompts are culturally sensitive, and students from varying backgrounds may not share the assumed prior experience needed to respond successfully. Many gifted and talented students overanalyze prompts and, in doing so, leave themselves little time to write their wonderful ideas in the test booklet. Of course many students simply struggle with writing in general. Add to all these reasons test anxiety and the pressure of writing on demand, and it's a wonder any students produce strong responses on their writing assessments.

No matter their skill or confidence level, no matter their background or the label on their IEP (Individualized Education Plan), if students don't feel a connection to the prompt that is supposed to spark their writing, their response is not likely to reflect their best abilities. We can't expect students to write creatively, to include evocative details, or to craft thoughtful paragraphs if they don't care about the subject. All students can benefit from a fun, easy, powerful way to connect writing prompts to their own lives.

Hope discovered the solution while watching her daughter Loren's drama class. The drama coach instructed the students to "become the scene" in order to understand it prior to acting it out. Children became birds, trees, squirrels, and even flowers. They became a living, breathing picture. Watching these young thespians, Hope realized that her young writers could "become the prompt" in language arts class in order to understand it before writing.

Thus, the prompt enactment process was born. Simply put: by acting out writing prompts, students train themselves to find personal connections with them. This helps them produce rich, creative writing. Just as a scene enactment helps an actor to emote, a prompt enactment helps students to write.

The process makes use of strategies that are as simple as a game of charades. Once students have the tools to actively become a part of writing prompts, their ideas can quickly flow. Fear and pressure evaporate.

The prompt enactment process has proven to be successful time and time again. We have used this process in our classrooms with our students and shared it at professional development workshops across our state. The response has been overwhelmingly positive. Students smile, greet us in the hallways, share their enactments, and invite us to listen as they communicate their stories orally. Teachers have embraced this approach. They tell us about their successes in person, on written evaluations, and through emails.

It's important to point out that this is not simply a "test prep" book. The prompt enactment process is about good writing. It can be used any time, throughout a writer's life, to produce stronger, more personal work. While we acknowledge that writing and test taking are two distinct tasks, the beauty of this process is that it helps students improve at *both*.

It's also important to note that doing enactments is not hard! It does not require acting talent, nerves of steel, or the memorization of scripts. We are not actors, only teachers who care about the success of kids. If you're intimidated by the phrase "performing arts," don't worry. This is low-key, low-stress, and fun. You'll see.

We wrote this book because we feel compelled to share our process with you; as fellow educators, we are all in the same boat. We invite you and your students to share your *See It, Be It, Write It* experiences with us. You may contact us by writing to us in care of our publisher:

Free Spirit Publishing
217 Fifth Avenue North, Suite 200
Minneapolis, MN 55401-1299
help4kids@freespirit.com

Break a leg!
Hope and Maryellen

Introduction

As mandated state assessments place more and more pressure on teachers and students alike, it's no longer enough to merely teach our students the elements of good writing. Students must perform on mandated state assessments. Because of this, in many classrooms, writing instruction has evolved into a series of test-driven writing responses scored with rubrics. But even with all the preparation and practice, some students still fall below the assessment benchmark. The irony is that some of these students are our very best writers. Why is this happening?

Children usually do best at what they enjoy doing most. It should come as no surprise that many students enjoy gym and art classes the most. When asked, our students said they enjoyed gym because they got to move around, they could make noise, and they could be on teams. They liked art because it was colorful, there was more than one right answer, and the teacher was like a coach giving directions and letting the kids do the rest on their own.

We have over fifty years of combined teaching experience, and we can honestly say that writing and test prep have never been favorites of our students or our peers. At best, they rank down there with word problems and rained-out recess. Unfortunately, many students not only dislike writing, they're actually intimidated by it. For them, state mandated writing assessments inspire fear, stress, even panic.

For many teachers and students, pressure to perform has turned a stimulating and often enjoyable learning process into one filled with anxiety. The role of the teacher often resembles more of a drill sergeant than a coach. Fewer students view writing as a means of communication or a vehicle for creative expression. For many, writing is simply a section on the dreaded test and leaves them wondering, "When will I ever use this?"

The Birth of a New Genre of Writing

Beginning in third grade and continuing through grade eleven, most students will spend a minimum of forty-five days in high-stakes assessment settings. The writing requirements and prompt responses on assessments have become so specific that this form of writing has evolved into its very own genre. Like all genres of writing, assessment writing requires a specific ensemble of skills and strategies in order to communicate to a specific audience for a specific reason. Your students must know that the writing process they demonstrate on assessments is no different from the writing process they use both inside and outside the classroom. Good writing is, quite simply, good writing.

But assessment writing is unique. What sets it apart is that the audience is made up of evaluators rather than just readers. This situation may be compared to a movie being viewed by a general audience one night, and then viewed by an audience of movie critics the next. Both sets of viewers will find things they like and dislike about the movie. The critics' opinions, however, will have a direct impact on the public relations and financial success of the movie.

Evaluators are looking for particular things. They want to see the demonstration of specific skills. Students writing for assessments must demonstrate those skills in order to obtain points. The more skills they demonstrate, the more points they accrue, and the higher their final score will be.

Yet writing—and writing instruction—is so much more than test prep! Writing provides a way for people to connect, and to feel connected, to themselves and to others. Writing is a powerful way of making oneself heard. It's a way for children to let others know who they are. Most students, if not all students, will need to write throughout their entire lives for both personal and professional reasons.

Writing is far more important than prompts and response sheets. We as educators must never forget that. Yes, we must prepare our students for the test. But we must also prepare them for their writing lives. With *See It, Be It, Write It,* you can do both.

Why Do Enactments?

This book explains the prompt enactment process, a strategy for teaching writing that consists of two basic parts:

1. Students enact a prompt. Physically acting out a prompt helps writers think more critically about it and compare their own experiences to it. They begin to think about the prompt in specific and personal ways. Later in the year, and well before the assessment, students learn to do this step in their heads.

2. With the aid of a Standing Ovation Checklist, students write a response to the prompt. The checklists in this book help them remember to include various writing techniques that are part of state assessment scoring rubrics and are elements of good writing in general. With practice, students internalize the writing techniques so they no longer need to refer to a hard copy.

Why do enactments? The prompt enactment process improves writing skills and performance on writing assessments. As we have seen from this new genre of writing, these are not necessarily identical, but they are of course both important. The prompt enactment process:

Helps students engage with writing assignments so they can write creatively, thoughtfully, and personally. Enactments bring writing prompts to life for students and connect the prompts to their background experiences, which helps them write responses with more detail—and more motivation and purpose.

Takes the mystery out of testing for kids. The Standing Ovation Checklists are directly aligned with state and national standards, including the Common Core Standards and state assessment scoring rubrics, yet they are presented in a user-friendly format. The checklists are very specific, taking the guesswork out of writing and scoring. Whether students are writing for a high-stakes assessment or a regular school assignment—even in curricular areas other than language arts—the checklists help them demonstrate all the writing techniques they have mastered. As the process becomes habit, your students will internalize the checklists. This is important during standardized testing situations when posters, rubrics, and visual aids may not be visible to the students.

Is easy to differentiate. Most classrooms contain students from a wide range of backgrounds and ability levels. It's the teacher's responsibility to reach all students where they *are*, and not where we think they should be. Since the prompt enactment process encourages students to make personal connections to writing prompts, it takes advantage of students' strengths and supports their weaknesses. And every part of the prompt enactment process can be differentiated readily, from enacting, to analyzing, to writing, to editing. This is covered in detail in Chapter 5: Differentiating the Enactment Process.

Is aligned with state standards and can be tailored to your state's assessment test. As you can see on the tables on pages 7–9, the prompt enactment process is aligned to state standards for language arts and national performing arts standards for states that have them. The Standing Ovation Checklists included in this book are aligned with

scoring rubrics used on real state assessment tests. This book has in-depth chapters on all the types of writing prompts that appear on state assessments, so you can easily focus on material your students need to know.

Supports social-emotional health. As your young writers take center stage to enact prompts, they learn to understand their own feelings as well as the feelings of others. Their self-esteem grows as they express themselves, improve their skills, and receive a sincere and appreciative round of applause after each enactment.

Is fun. Kids doing prompt enactments are actively learning. They move around, they laugh, they share ideas. They might even act silly. Active learning not only is a great way to retain information, it is more fun than passive learning!

About This Book

See It, Be It, Write It is divided into four sections.

Part 1: Using Performing Arts to Improve Writing Skills and Test Scores. This part summarizes the prompt enactment process and explains how to use it throughout your year. We recommend you read all of the chapters in Part 1 to gain a strong sense of how to use the process.

Part 2: Extending and Optimizing the Process. This part guides you in differentiating the process so you can engage all your learners; offers plenty of easy ways to take enactments further if you so desire (with sets, scriptwriting, costumes, and more); and describes the social-emotional learning (SEL) benefits of enactments (including specific SEL-based activities). Reading Part 2 will help you get the most out of the prompt enactment process.

Part 3: The Types of Writing Prompts. Each chapter in this part explains in detail one of the types of writing prompts found on state assessments: picture, speculative, persuasive, poetry, and quote or adage prompts. The chapters show you precisely how to do the prompt enactment process with each type of writing prompt, providing examples and plenty of tips for directing a smooth performance. Each chapter in Part 3 also contains a prompt-specific version of the Standing Ovation Checklist. We recommend you read the chapter or chapters that correspond with the prompt types your students will find on their assessment.

Part 4: Ready-to-Use Prompts. This part provides—you guessed it—ready-to-use writing prompts. You'll find five prompts for each of the five types, complete with discussion questions and suggestions for enacting.

You'll also find five themed assignments that contain one writing prompt for each of the different prompt types based on the same subject matter, as well as suggestions for extending and differentiating the theme. These prompts are complete and ready to be printed out and put into use right away. (We also encourage you—or your students—to design your own prompts.)

Throughout this book you will find "Director's Notes," which are asides to you, the director of the big prompt-enacting and writing show in your classroom. Director's Notes provide additional important information about the topic at hand.

Also included with this book is a CD-ROM, on which you'll find all seventy-six of the reproducible handouts in the book (plus twenty more reproducible student prompts not in the book). All the forms are in PDF format. Many of these, including forms for planning and organizing your year, are customizable with fields you can fill in on screen. Having electronic copies of the various versions of the Standing Ovation Checklist can be quite handy when you need to print out copies for every student in your class.

The best thing about *See It, Be It, Write It* is that you won't need to reinvent the wheel. This process helps kids, whatever their writing ability or confidence level, to take ownership of their writing—whether they are writing for class, for a state assessment, or for themselves.

Part 1

Using Performing
Arts to Improve Writing
Skills and Test Scores

Chapter 1
Standards, Assessments, and Getting to Know Your Students

Through the prompt enactment process, you and your students will take a journey of writing instruction that will help them become stronger, more competent writers—in your classroom and beyond. Early in the school year, your journey begins with the creation of a lively, collaborative learning atmosphere. You and your students will work together enacting and discussing prompts, writing responses, and revising. As the year goes on, the fun, collaborative spirit continues even as students take on more of the work themselves. By the end of the year, as the testing date approaches, students will need to do the enactment process all on their own—and not only on their own, but inside their heads!

The Enactment Process and State Standards

In addition to helping your students improve as writers and preparing them for your state assessment, it's also important to note that the enactment process itself satisfies curriculum standards for writing, speaking and listening, and theater. The enactment process is not something extra to do—it is a new way to teach what you're already doing. The process directly involves the teacher and the student in speaking, listening, writing, and reading in ways that promote a student's ability to communicate successfully.

The tables on pages 7–9 shows exactly how the enactment process addresses typical language arts curriculum standards. The standards provided include standards for two representative states, California and Texas. Your own state's standards are likely very similar.

Director's Note
Forty-eight states have agreed to participate in the establishment of Common Core Standards, the goal of which is to establish more uniform expectations for the nation's students. Based on drafts made available in 2009 and the current process to establish these standards, we are confident the enactment process will align with the Common Core Standards. 🎭

The prompt enactment process also satisfies state and national standards for arts education. The following national standards were developed by the Consortium of National Arts Education Associations.

Aligning the Enactment Process with State Language Arts Standards

Addressed during the Enactment Process	California	Texas
Students focus on the beginning, then on the middle, and finally on the end of their enactments and their written stories; students and teachers talk through what could have happened before and after the moment they enact; when speaking and scribing, teachers and students use transition words to discuss chronology.	Listening and Speaking Strategies, 1.5 and 1.6 (Organization and Delivery): Organize ideas chronologically or around major points of information. Provide a beginning, a middle, and an end, including concrete details that develop a central idea.	Beginning in 4th grade, students are expected to develop drafts by choosing an appropriate organizational strategy (e.g., sequence of events, cause effect, compare contrast) and building on ideas to create a focused, organized, and coherent piece of writing.
Conventions of written English are discussed and practiced during discussions about enactments, teacher scribing, student writing, and especially when using the Standing Ovation Checklist to compose and edit.	Written and Oral English Language Conventions, 1.0: Students write and speak with a command of standard English conventions appropriate to this grade level.	Beginning in 4th grade, students are expected to edit drafts for grammar, mechanics, and spelling using a teacher developed rubric.
Writers are taught various strategies to engage readers, including using hooks and drafting sentences that use question marks and exclamation points.	Written and Oral English Language Conventions, 1.1 (Sentence Structure): Understand and be able to use complete and correct declarative, interrogative, imperative, and exclamatory sentences in writing and speaking.	Beginning in 5th grade, students are expected to use a variety of sentence structures and transitions to link paragraphs.
Students practice using precise vocabulary through exercises like "Put *said* to bed" and the 5 synonym switch.	Writing Strategies, 1.5 (Research and Technology): Use a thesaurus to identify alternative word choices and meanings.	
Students learn to recognize the writing task by analyzing writing prompts and practice writing appropriate responses, keeping the audience in mind; students practice using precise vocabulary; students are encouraged to write "fan mail" to other students as well as write and send persuasive letters.	Writing Strategies, 1.0: Students write clear, coherent, and focused essays. The writing exhibits the students' awareness of the audience and purpose. Essays contain formal introductions, supporting evidence, and conclusions.	Beginning in 4th grade, students are expected to write letters whose language is tailored to the audience and purpose (e.g., a thank-you note to a friend) and that use appropriate conventions (e.g., date, salutation, closing).

Texas Essential Knowledge and Skills for English Electives © 2009 by the Texas Education Agency. Reprinted with permission.

English-Language Arts Content Standards for California Public Schools: Kindergarten Through Grade Twelve © 1997 by the California State Board of Education. Reprinted with permission.

Aligning the Enactment Process with State Language Arts Standards
(continued)

Addressed during the Enactment Process	California	Texas
Students learn to write in various genres and to stay on topic by participating in scribing sessions, and later they practice it in their own writing and edit it using a Standing Ovation Checklist. Clear focus and strong supporting details are stressed at every stage of the process.	Writing Applications, 2.0: Students write narrative, expository, persuasive, and descriptive texts of at least 500 to 700 words in each genre. Student writing demonstrates a command of standard American English and the research, organizational, and drafting strategies.	Students write expository and procedural or work-related texts to communicate ideas and information to specific audiences for specific purposes. Beginning in 3rd grade, students are expected to write brief compositions that contain a clear focus, organization, and sufficient supporting details.
Students may work on poetry prompts when appropriate; the enactment process is also appropriate for cross-curricular writing, and specific instruction for doing so is included in this book.	Literary Response and Analysis, 3.0: Students read and respond to historically or culturally significant works of literature that reflect and enhance their studies of history and social science. They clarify the ideas and connect them to other literary works.	
The audience discusses the enactment with the actors; students discuss the enactment and the writing with the teacher during scribing sessions; students have many opportunities to work in groups on enacting, writing, and editing.	Listening and Speaking 1.0, Comprehension: Ask questions that seek information not already discussed.	Students work productively with others in teams. Beginning in 3rd grade, students are expected to participate in teacher- and student-led small-group discussions by posing and answering questions with appropriate detail and providing suggestions that build upon the ideas of others.
Students may practice standard English as well as the expression of ideas and feelings when doing enactments, during discussions, during scribing sessions, when writing responses, and when editing, particularly when editing with the Standing Ovation Checklists.	Written and Oral English Language Conventions, 1.0: Students write and speak with a command of standard English conventions appropriate to this grade level.	Beginning in 3rd grade, students are expected to write imaginative stories that build the plot to a climax and contain details about the characters and setting. Students write literary texts to express their ideas and feelings about real or imagined people, events, and ideas.
Students brainstorm for essays during enactments, visualization, and discussions; they draft essays and revise them using the Standing Ovation Checklist.	Writing Strategies, 1.4 (Evaluation and Revision): Students revise drafts to improve the coherence and logical progression of ideas by using an established rubric.	Students use elements of the writing process (planning, drafting, revising, editing, and publishing) to compose text. Beginning in 2nd grade, students are expected to edit drafts for grammar, punctuation, and spelling using a teacher developed rubric.

National Standards for Arts Education

Theatre, Content Standard 2, Achievement Standard: Students imagine and clearly describe characters, their relationships, and their environments

Theatre, Content Standard 1, Achievement Standard: Students improvise dialogue to tell stories, and formalize improvisations by writing or recording the dialogue

Theatre, Content Standard 1, Achievement Standard: Students refine and record dialogue and action

Theatre, Content Standard 2, Achievement Standard: Students in an ensemble, create and sustain characters that communicate with audiences

Theatre, Content Standard 1, Achievement Standard: Script writing by the creation of improvisations and scripted scenes based on personal experience and heritage, imagination, literature, and history

Theatre, Content Standard 7, Achievement Standard: Students analyze classroom dramatizations and, using appropriate terminology, constructively suggest alternative ideas for dramatizing roles, arranging environments, and developing situations along with means of improving the collaborative processes of planning, playing, responding, and evaluating

Theatre, Content Standard 6, Achievement Standard: Students express and compare personal reactions to several art forms

Visual Arts, Content Standard 5: Reflecting upon and assessing the characteristics and merits of their work and the work of others

National Standards for Theatre Education © 2001 by the American Alliance for Theatre & Education. Reprinted with permission.

Getting to Know Your State Assessment

Early in the year, your students don't need to worry about the assessment they'll take at the end of the year, but you do. Though good writing skills are appropriate for any writing occasion, you don't want your students to be surprised by what they find on the test. Therefore, you'll use the contents of your state's assessment test to help determine the structure of your yearlong writing program.

The contents of your state's assessment test are based on your state's writing standards, which you can access at the department of education (DOE) Web site for your state. (You can also find links to each state's standards at www .educationworld.com.) Although many states are involved in the process of establishing Common Core Standards, individual states will maintain control over their assessments

and the terminology used to identify and describe different purposes for writing. Even if your state adopts the Common Core Standards, the best place to learn about your state assessment test is from your state DOE.

To find the information on your state's DOE Web site, look for a tab or button labeled "Assessment." After finding the assessment section, locate the particular grade and name of your state's test. You may find a section labeled "Test Item Specifications" or something similar, and that is where you will be able to read about the types of questions, the quantity of questions, and the length of time students have to respond to the assessment tasks. You will not be able to preview specific prompts for the current year, of course, however you may find prompts from previous years, which can be very valuable (see pages 43–45). You will also be able to find information about the types of writing prompts by regularly checking the DOE Web site for postings related to the high stakes assessment; look for presentations, multimedia slides, and official notifications.

A brief description of prompt types

Keep in mind that like the standards themselves, the terminology used to describe types of writing, the names of assessment prompts, and their targeted grade levels will vary from state to state. Use the chart on this page to help match up your states terminology with that used in this book.

Picture prompt

The picture prompt requires students to look at an illustration or photo, make keen observations, and incorporate their observations and thoughts into a creatively written story. The students must demonstrate their ability to apply creative writing skills while crafting their story.

Speculative prompt

The speculative prompt requires students to read a brief scenario, make a personal connection to the scenario, and craft a story that includes a resolution to the scenario. Speculative prompts sometimes include social-emotional skill-building strategies and moral dilemmas. Similar to the picture prompt, this task allows the students to demonstrate their ability to write creatively.

Persuasive prompt

The persuasive prompt requires students to take a stance on a given topic or situation. Their task is to include details from their experiences, or information they have learned during class lessons or from other sources, in order to persuade the reader to agree with their position. Persuasive prompts often require students to respond in the form of a friendly letter.

Poetry prompt

The poetry prompt requires students to respond to a poem. A teacher reads the poem aloud, and students read it silently. The students do not write a poem. Their assignment is to make a connection to the main idea of the poem and include that connection in their written response. They must be sure to respond to questions related to the main idea and theme of the poem. Evaluators are looking for a text-to-text, text-to-self, or text-to-world connection.

Quote or adage prompt

The quote or adage prompt requires students to respond to a quote. A teacher reads the quote aloud, and the students read it silently. The students must grasp the main idea or message of the quote and connect that message to a personal experience. Students must

Terms Commonly Used on State Assessments (Jargon Conversion Table)

If it says	This book says
Visual stimulus or visual narrative prompt	Picture prompt
Personal narrative or writing to convey experience, real or imagined	Story (in response to a picture prompt or speculative prompt)
Argument, argumentative writing, or convincing writing	Persuasive writing (or persuasive prompt)
Narrative in response to a variety of stimulus materials, explanatory writing, expository writing	Written response (to a poetry prompt or quote or adage prompt)
Benchmarks	Mastery level
Proficiency levels: • Basic • Proficient • Advanced	Proficiency levels: • Partially Proficient • Proficient • Advanced Proficient
Composition or essay	Written response
Narrative writing	Story

respond to questions following the quote and demonstrate their ability to make connections and to write about a lesson they have learned or might learn from such an experience. As with the poetry prompt, evaluators are looking for a text-to-text, text-to-self, or text-to-world connection.

You can collect everything you need to know about your state's test on a copy of the "Writing Assessment Information Fact Sheet," on page 12. You will also want to check into your state's DOE Web site regularly for updates on test dates, sample prompts, and important test information.

Getting to Know Your Students

Once you've gathered the information you need about your standards and your assessment, you'll want to find out what kind of writers you have in your classroom. If an assessment was given last year, find out what each student scored on it. You may locate the results in the students' cumulative folder or in an online database; many states have tracking systems that give educators access to the records of students who have transferred within districts, between districts, and from state to state or province to province.

Whenever possible, visit the resident sage, last year's teacher, to gain further insight into your students' strengths and weaknesses. Working together will save valuable time and give you a deeper understanding of each student's individual needs. By itself, a test score does not represent a student. It is never enough!

Collect the prior test scores and any other information you can gather from the previous teachers for each student in your class on the "Previous Writing Test Data Collection Sheet" (page 13). You will be able to sort students by score and also categorize them by mastery levels.

Once you have collected data for all your students, use the "Assessment Writing Clusters" chart (page 14) to group your students for appropriate instruction. This is one method of addressing specific needs of groups of students and using test data to make instructional decisions. Don't consider these groups set in stone for the entire school year. Please note that due to each

state's control over word choices, the terminology may be different in your state than the terminology used in this chart. In New Jersey, we use the terms *advanced proficient, proficient,* and *partial proficient* to indicate levels of mastery. Please adapt the categories in this chart to reflect the names of the levels of mastery in your state.

Director's Note
A customizable version of each of these charts is included on the CD-ROM, so you can fill in your state's specific terminology. 🎭

In some school districts, teachers collect and maintain samples of their students' writings at different intervals during the school year. These documents are placed in a writing folder that is passed along to the next year's teacher. Teachers may use these samples as a preview of their students' abilities and prior mastery to prepare for future remedial and/or instructional lessons. Prompt responses are ideal writing samples to be placed in students' writing folders.

The "Student Progressive Writing Chart" on page 15 may be used as a cover page for each student's writing folder. It shows what writing prompts each student has been exposed to. You may mark an X in the appropriate square when the student is exposed to the given prompt, or, to be more specific, you may include a date when that lesson began. For your convenience, you may collect your entire class's information on the "Class Progressive Writing Chart" on page 16.

Writing Assessment Information Fact Sheet

Name of state assessment: _____

State Department of Education Web site: _____

Name of the District Testing Coordinator: _____ Email: _____

Name of School-based Testing Coordinator: _____ Email: _____

Dates and times assessment will be given:

Day of Week	Date	Time

Types of Writing Prompts included on assessment:

Name of Writing Prompt	Description of Prompt	Date of Instruction

Names of students needing special accommodations during assessment:

Name of Student	Accommodation(s) Needed

Prior to the assessment, have you:

- Checked your state's Department of Education Web site for assessment information and updates?
- Taken down/covered all educational aides from walls, etc?
- Reviewed IEPs/classified student educational plans?
- Made arrangements for testing accommodations?
- Rearranged classroom furniture as per testing protocols?
- Obtained two #2 pencils for each student?
- Obtained a functioning clock/timer?

Previous Writing Test Data Collection Sheet

Student's Name	Name of Test	Date of Test	Type of Prompt	Score on Writing Section	Mastery Level
1.					
2.					
3.					
4.					
5.					
6.					
7.					
8.					
9.					
10.					
11.					
12.					
13.					
14.					
15.					
16.					
17.					
18.					
19.					
20.					
21.					
22.					
23.					
24.					
25.					
26.					
27.					
28.					
29.					
30.					

Assessment Writing Clusters

Cluster 1: Students with Advanced Proficient Writing Scores

Cluster 2: Students with Proficient Writing Scores

Cluster 3: Students with Partial Proficient Writing Scores

Student Progressive Writing Chart

Student's name: _____

Date and grade student began in the school system: _____

	Picture Prompt	Speculative Prompt	Persuasive Prompt	Poetry Prompt	Quote/Adage Prompt
1st-grade teacher:					
2nd-grade teacher:					
3rd-grade teacher:					
4th-grade teacher:					
5th-grade teacher:					
6th-grade teacher:					
7th-grade teacher:					
8th-grade teacher:					
9th-grade teacher:					
10th-grade teacher:					
11th-grade teacher:					
12th-grade teacher:					

Comments:

_____

_____

_____

_____

Class Progressive Writing Chart

Information from each individual Student Progressive Writing Chart may be applied to the chart below to aid in your yearlong planning for writing instruction.

Student's Name	Picture Prompt	Specu-lative Prompt	Persuasive Prompt	Poetry Prompt	Quote/ Adage Prompt

Chapter 2
The Prompt Enactment Process

The prompt enactment process includes two phases: enacting and writing. This chapter describes the process in detail, using a picture prompt as an example, to provide you with a base from which to adapt your own process.

The first time you do the enactment process with your class, no matter whether they are third graders or eighth graders, we strongly encourage you to do two things:

1. Use a picture prompt even if your state does not include a picture prompt on its assessment for your grade. It is the easiest prompt to introduce the process, since students can easily make a visual connection and they have an obvious starting point for enacting. It is the easiest prompt type to write about, so students can focus on the process and get used to making personal connections to writing prompts without worrying about more complicated writing requirements.

2. Scribe the written response together as a class rather than requiring students to write their own responses.

After you do the enactment process the first time with your class, you will need to decide—based on what you know about your students' skills—what kind of writing prompt to use in subsequent writing occasions and whether to scribe any, part, or all of a response. See Chapter 4: Encore Performances for help.

Director's Note

Before your first enactment assignment, you may wish to show the movie *Mary Poppins* to your class—specifically the scene in which the actors jump into the chalk drawing on a sidewalk. This scene gives students a frame of reference for "bringing a picture to life." It shows the transformation of something that is two-dimensional becoming something that is living and breathing, something three-dimensional. Another good example is the Broadway show *Sunday in the Park with George,* in which the famous Seurat painting comes to life. 🎭

Step 1: View the Prompt

Display the prompt so everyone in your class is able to see it clearly and easily. If you are working with a large group, you may wish to project the prompt with a computer or projector. Instruct your students to study the prompt silently for two minutes.

In this chapter, we use the "Lemonade Stand" picture prompt as an example, but see pages 78–79 for ideas on finding prompts that will engage your students. For written prompts, read the prompt aloud to your class before asking them to read it.

Step 2: Discuss the Prompt

After two minutes, ask your students who and what they see in the picture and actively listen to their responses. A great way to start this discussion is by asking your students to answer the following question: If this picture could talk, who would be talking and what would we hear? You may even go so far as to put the picture up to your ear or, if you are projecting the picture on a screen, cup your hand to your ear near the image as if you are listening to it. This emphasizes the point that the picture really does have something to say, we just have to listen.

This is a preliminary discussion, a brainstorming opportunity. There are no right or wrong answers. What students verbalize now may or may not be what they write at the end of the process. This discussion is a way to help your students start thinking critically about the prompt. Try to keep it lively and nonjudgmental. The true beauty of art is the individual interpretations it elicits. This part of the process also serves as a perfect vehicle to invite diverse ideas and create an inclusive atmosphere in your classroom.

Step 3: Enact the Prompt

Following the discussion, and with the image still in view, ask for volunteers to become actors. Pointing to the prompt, announce to your actors that they are going to breathe life into this picture. Tell them that they will bring this picture from flat (two-dimensional) to fabulous (three-dimensional). Once you have your volunteers, without further direction, ask them to enact the prompt—in other words, to become the picture. For this first time, and perhaps for subsequent times, they will simply re-create the scene in the picture without using dialogue. As your class gets more experienced, you may add dialogue, action, props, set pieces, and more (see chapters 4 and 6). The first time, though, it is best to keep it simple and nonintimidating.

Director's Note

Start with kids who are comfortable performing in front of their classmates. Once your students understand that this is a fun and nonjudgmental exercise, many more will want to "get in on the act." Keep in mind that one of the goals of a prompt enactment is for your students to have fun! Giggles are contagious and welcomed. 🎭

Give the actors a minute to discuss among themselves who will take which roles, what they should do, and so on. Tell the rest of the students in your class to assume the role of an "active audience." Their job is to observe the enactment in order to answer the question, "What is happening in this picture?"

Here's an example of what one of our prompt enactments looked like:

Be It

Your students' role as audience members is that of active observers. This role must be clearly defined. Tell your audience members they should do the following during the enactment:

1. Listen intently.

2. Stay seated during the entire enactment. They are not to raise a hand or ask to leave the room unless it is an emergency.

3. Think about what the actors are doing well. Absolutely no negative comments, gestures, or facial expressions are allowed.

4. Think about how this enactment makes them feel. Can they identify with the characters (imagine what they are feeling)?

5. Consider how they would have done the enactment differently. This may be the basis of the writing to follow.

Step 4: Discuss the Enactment

Once volunteers have silently enacted the prompt, ask them to remain positioned in the prompt for as long as they are comfortable. Ask audience members to comment on the enactment. Are they able to see the connection to the picture? Ask the actors if they feel connected to the scene in the picture.

Making a personal connection to the prompt

Strong writing exhibits a strong personal connection between the author and subject matter, and a personal connection is something assessment evaluators look for when reading students' written responses. This is one of the main benefits of the prompt enactment process: doing prompt enactments helps students put themselves into the prompt and make the necessary connection. During this discussion phase of the process, encourage your students to think of how they might make a connection to the prompt.

Text-to-self connection

The most obvious and likely connections for students is between the writing prompt and their own experience. Ask students to think of any personal experiences the writing prompt reminds them of. For example, using our lemonade stand theme, students could think about and share their experiences tasting lemonade, making lemonade, or selling lemonade or iced tea. If they haven't sold lemonade, they may have sold something else, such as cookies for Girl Scouts, popcorn for Boy Scouts, or books for a school fundraiser.

Text-to-text connection

Those students who have not had personal experiences related to the theme of the writing prompt may have read stories or seen movies in which that theme was explored. Perhaps they've read about characters who had lemonade sales or garage sales, for example. Students can use what they have read or watched as a source for ideas and fodder for details.

Text-to-world connection

This refers to a connection between the writing prompt and the community at large. The connections can be with people, places, or events outside of their personal realm. For example, a student who knows about a recent natural disaster may wish to have the characters in his or her response use their lemonade profit to buy books for children who live in the area affected by the event. If your community is involved in an election, a major sporting or arts event, a crisis, or a fair or festival, just to name a few examples, these all may become part of a text-to-world connection for one or more of your writers.

Director's Note

Since it may be difficult to remain in position for a period of time, you may want to use a camera to capture the enactment scene. This enables you to retrieve the scene should the actors become tired and it also lets you and the students use it for reference at a later time. If you use a digital camera, you can display the picture immediately after taking it, either on the computer screen or by projecting it.

Once you have several of these digital photos, they will be great additions to a classroom "Prompt Enactment Scrapbook" or hallway bulletin board. 🎭

Next, ask the students in the audience to generate and share as many appropriate verbal reactions to the enacted prompt as possible. Be sure to support your students' ideas so that each child is encouraged to share as many feelings and first-impressions as possible. You may write student responses on the board or chart paper, if desired.

Soon, you will want to begin to focus the discussion. Dialogue and detail are great ways to enhance stories, and now is the time to encourage your students to suggest ideas for both. If they have made some sort of personal connection to the prompt, they may be able to mine their personal experience for these ideas. You may also encourage students to enact dialogue or details if that helps them flesh out their ideas.

A good way to encourage as well as narrow the discussion is with the following discussion questions:

- Who are the characters? What are their names? Don't allow students to use the names of classmates for these characters. You don't want to turn this into a popularity contest, nor do you want to make anyone feel uncomfortable.

- Decide who is speaking first. Ask the students to explain their choices. These explanations will build responses that convey focused attention to the details in the enactment.

- What do you think the characters are saying to each other?

- What are the characters doing? Why are they doing this?

- Are they happy or sad?

- Where do you think this lemonade stand is located?

- How did they make the lemonade (what happened before)?

- What will they do with the money they make selling their lemonade (what will happen next)?

These questions are formed from the first part of the Standing Ovation Checklist for picture prompts on page 82. Keep this list handy while you are directing your discussion so that these topics are covered by your class. The list is a great guide for class discussions, and you will read much more about the Standing Ovation Checklists in chapter 3.

For older students and/or highly capable students, you may go beyond the checklists and ask more abstract questions or questions that require greater leaps of imagination or logic. Typical questions for the lemonade stand prompt might include:

- What could be added to the prompt to make it more interesting?

- What could be taken away from the prompt to make it more interesting?

- How could they stay in business if it started to rain?

- What could one character say or do to persuade the other character to use the money the way he or she wants?

- What song could you include as background music for the enactment? What song could be used as part of the enactment?

- How could you persuade your principal to allow you to have a school-wide lemonade sale?

- How could you include a television commercial or magazine ad in your enactment?

After you have a good collection of ideas, you will need to decide which ones to keep for your group's story. One way to make these decisions is by voting. Votes may be conducted in a variety of ways, a few of which are described on page 29. Have students vote with their eyes closed so no one is influenced to cast a certain vote.

Step 5: A Round of Applause
Celebrating the Process

At the end of the prompt enactment, have your audience reward the actors with an enthusiastic round of applause. This is a critical step to include after *every* enactment as a means of congratulations for a job well done.

The round of applause is meant to be sincere and brief and have an air of encouragement and appreciation. A sincere round of applause can forge a sense of camaraderie and a sense of achievement among the classmates. You might want to create a signal to begin and end a round of applause. You are an integral part of the round of applause, so please participate along with your students.

Director's Note

For many students, these classroom scenes may be their first foray into speaking and acting in front of anyone. The round of applause is very important to help boost the confidence of these students. Keep your eyes and ears open—you may find some hidden talent among your troupe. Skills and strategies related to choreography, staging, voice projection, and visualization will transcend the content areas and filter into many careers. Who knows? If students are encouraged and confident, prompt enactments may inspire them to become future actors, directors, set designers, or scriptwriters. 🎭

Fan Mail

To encourage audience members to support those brave volunteers who enacted the prompt, suggest (or even require) that they write fan mail to a specific actor (or the entire cast) telling what they liked about the performance. Instruct them to give details to support their comments. Collect the fan mail in order to make sure that each note is appropriate and positive. Once you have read them, deliver them to the addressees. Depending on the age, experience, and confidence of your writers, you can have them write an original note or use the following template.

Here's a sample fan mail letter using the template:

Date_____

Dear _____,

I really enjoyed _____

_____

_____

Bravo!

_____

January 20

Dear Dexter,
I really enjoyed the way you moved like an old man during the enactment. The man in the picture looks like my grandfather and he walks just like you did.

Bravo!
Taylor

Fan mail is always popular with students. It is a wonderful way to build confidence and self-esteem for your actors, and it's a fun writing task for audience members. They love receiving these notes.

Step 6: Write or Scribe a Prompt Response

Following the prompt enactment, direct the actors and audience to look once again at the original picture prompt. This return focus helps them get ready to write. For your first time or first few times, scribe the writing together as a group. Compose the beginning, middle, and end of the text. This part of the process evolves as your students become more confident and secure with their ability to write prompt responses. In classes of all grade levels, the transition from "the teacher as the scribe" to "the student as the writer" occurs in a series of stages that you will have to orchestrate. See Chapter 4: Encore Performances for more about transitioning to student as writer.

We have found that chart paper is the most effective writing medium to use when scribing with students, even if the classroom is filled with the latest technology tools. Working together in a close group, producing words with marker and paper, cultivates a collaborative writing relationship. Students feel more encouraged to suggest ideas. At this point, the onus of writing is not on their shoulders. They have the freedom to contribute as you become their secretary, their scribe. Like the class discussion earlier in the process, try to keep the tone light and upbeat. As students offer more ideas—and as their ideas flow faster—it can be fun to act like you are writing at a frenetic pace. Play it up for a few moments and then say, "Whew! You have so many great ideas, we could write a whole book."

Another great thing about chart paper, especially pads that have self-sticking tops, is that you can display the finished pages. Students can use the pages as reminders the next time they write. Hanging it in a "place of honor," either inside your classroom or in the halls, also sets the stage for your students to be proud of their finished product. While displaying the pages for later viewing works best if you have your own classroom, teachers who share rooms might wish to layer the pages so they become a large flip book.

We recommend you divide your scribing into three sessions—the beginning, the middle, and the end—in order to avoid burnout. Schedule scribing sessions on subsequent days or with a maximum of two days between each session to keep the momentum going (and the enactment fresh in students' minds).

Begin each session by reviewing the enactment and refocusing on the original prompt.

The first session: the story begins

In your first session, you will scribe the beginning of the story. Depending on the age and skill level of your students, the opening may be one short paragraph or much longer. The seeds for the written response were planted during your enactment and especially during the discussion afterward. As you get ready to begin scribing the beginning, recap the enactment, the discussion, and the ideas you agreed on. Then begin to write the story on the chart, modeling for your students how to take their ideas and decisions and turn them into well-written sentences that convey the hook for the story. For younger students, you will also be modeling:

- indenting paragraphs
- printing from left to right
- proper letter formation

Here is one way you might recap your first scribing session:

"We just acted out the picture. You brought the picture to life. Now, let's look at the picture prompt again and think about our discussion. We named our characters." Remind them of the names. "We agreed on a setting." Remind them of the setting. "We also decided what these characters' conflict is and who is speaking first." Remind them of what you decided. "Now we will put this all together to create our hook."

After you have scribed the story opening, the hook, have the class chorally read it. This group reading builds fluency skills and underscores the united class effort. Students feel part of a team as they begin to feel collective ownership of the story. After reading, have the students give themselves a round of applause. Finally, post this part of the story for the students to look at during the rest of the day. You might want to encourage students to mull over the story, jot ideas for the next part of the story on sticky notes, and place the notes on the paper throughout the day.

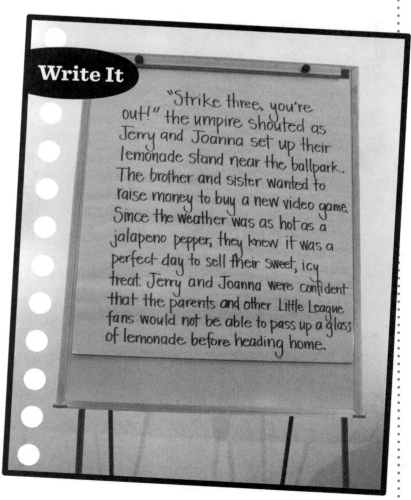

Write It

"Strike three, you're out!" the umpire shouted as Jerry and Joanna set up their lemonade stand near the ballpark. The brother and sister wanted to raise money to buy a new video game. Since the weather was as hot as a jalapeno pepper, they knew it was a perfect day to sell their sweet, icy treat. Jerry and Joanna were confident that the parents and other Little League fans would not be able to pass up a glass of lemonade before heading home.

The second session: the story evolves

During the second scribing session, you will build the middle of the story. Start by doing a choral reading of the beginning of the story and asking your students to look at the picture again. Recap what you decided during the discussion you had after the enactment. Keeping in mind what has already been written and discussed, you may read aloud any ideas written on sticky notes and discuss with your group how or if these ideas might be incorporated into your story. This step validates some of the students' ideas and may bring out their concerns or confusions, as well as add personal insights and ideas.

Now, move onto the middle of your story. What did the characters do to try to resolve their conflict? What happened as a result of that? What did the characters see, hear, taste, touch, and smell during the enactment? As you work with the group, focus on the following items from the Standing Ovation Checklist (again, please read chapter 3 for a more thorough discussion of the list and these items):

- Encourage use of the five senses as a springboard for adjectives and strong verbs.

- If your story opening doesn't have any metaphors or similes, the middle section is a good place to use one.

- If your hook did not include an onomatopoeia, the middle of the story is a good place to use it.

- Although personification may be used in the beginning, middle, or end, try to incorporate that element before you and the kids forget.

These four bulleted elements can be remembered with the acronym 5 MOPS, which stands for the **5** senses, **M**etaphor, **O**nomatopoeia, **P**ersonification, and **S**imile. The 5 MOPS do not need to appear in order; the acronym simply is an easy way to remember to include these elements where appropriate. It's a teacher and student tool.

You might start your second scribing session by saying:

"So far we have created the beginning of our story. Now, we're going to add details to make our story livelier and more colorful for our reader. This is something good writers do. To do this, we will start by using the 5 MOPS strategy. Look at the picture and reread the beginning of our story. Think about what the characters may be seeing, hearing, touching, tasting, and smelling at this time and in this location."

Get some suggestions and decide which to use. Add sentences using those details, reading aloud as you write.

"We have so much to say from the five senses. Where can we show the reader an image using a metaphor or a simile?" As before, get suggestions, choose which to use, and add them to your story. "I see a great place for onomatopoeia. Can you find a place for a sound word?"

Once you have completed the middle of your story, have the students give themselves a round of applause. Post this part of the story for the students to look at during the rest of the day. If you did so the previous session, encourage students to add ideas throughout the day for the next part of the story on sticky notes placed on the paper.

The third session: the story ends

During the third scribing session, bring the story to its conclusion. To make sure you use all the checklist elements, keep the Standing Ovation Checklist handy as your writing guide.

Start by rereading aloud the beginning and middle of the story and asking your students to look at the picture again. Recap what you decided during the discussion after the enactment, then talk with the class about what has happened in the story so far and how the story might end. You may read aloud

the ideas written on sticky notes and discuss adding them to your story. Emphasize that it is important to the reader that you bring the story to a conclusion by resolving the conflict (either positively or negatively) and not by writing the words "The End."

In this final section, encourage students to bring their skills full circle by including the final thoughts or spoken words of one of the characters. After you have finished scribing the end of the story, affirm students for their collaborative efforts. Review what they did that was positive; give a pat on the back for a job well done and acknowledge how challenging this can be at first and how they were able to succeed.

You might introduce your final scribing session this way:

"So far we have created the beginning and middle of our story. You have made choices about the setting, the names of the characters, the action, and many details. You have included a metaphor (or simile or onomatopoeia). Now it is time to wrap up our story.

"Look at the prompt, think back to the enactment, and reread the story so far. How might we conclude this story? What will happen after all that happened in our story so far? How will that resolve the conflict? Let's be sure to include a character's final thoughts or feelings: what do you think is the last thing this character will say?"

Finally, take a deep breath and together read the whole story out loud. When you're done, pause to reflect upon it. Tell the students to reread it silently to themselves with the purpose of thinking of a title for the story. Depending upon how much you have already taught the students about titles, you may need to explain that a good title is descriptive and interesting. You may also say that the story drives the title, rather than the title driving the story. That is the reason for reading it out loud and also silently. This is why the title as a writing response element appears at the end of the Standing Ovation Checklist.

One way to choose your title is to have students write their suggestions on pieces of paper and submit their ideas by putting the paper into a box. Review the slips of paper, select three title options, and read them aloud. After you read them, print them on the board and conduct a vote. The voting may be a show of hands or thumbs up/thumbs down. Have students cast their votes with their eyes closed so that individual choices are not influenced by peer responses. Alternatively, you could select three choices and print them on a copy of the story that you hand out the next day. Again, have students vote by a show of hands or thumbs.

Now that the story is complete, have the students give themselves a round of applause. Post the final sheet next to the other two sheets, leaving the entire story up for students and class guests to view. You might want to type it up to share with others and to keep for future use.

Self-Editing

After the first draft of a prompt response is scribed, it's time for students to edit their work. They should reread their draft carefully, using the Standing Ovation Checklist as a guide (see chapter 3). Have they included every element from the list in their piece? How is their penmanship? Have they indented each paragraph? Finally, they should do the 5 synonym switch (see page 32).

When you are scribing for the class, you will want to edit together. This can be especially instructive for students struggling with the process, since they see mistakes corrected and flat writing improved. Writing is not something that people do perfectly the first time. It is a process. When students are working alone on their own writing, they can do this editing independently or by trading with a partner.

Modifying the Process

As the year goes on and your students begin to show mastery of the process, you will modify the amount of scribing you do. Be sure to read Chapter 4: Encore Performances to learn about scribing and guiding the students to become independent prompt response writers. Of course the ultimate goal is for your students to write effectively without you. Eventually, your scribing phase will not be needed for most students. They will be able to write a response to the prompt completely on their own.

Director's Note
Scribing is an effective tool for English language learners, special needs students, including those on the Autism spectrum, and those students who simply need more time to master the process. This modeling process provides the students with a visual stimulus that matches what you say during the enactment process. They can look at it and see neat handwriting and the use of speech tags, onomatopoeia, and the names of characters. They can see the capital letters in the names of the characters and the punctuation marks you use. Also, your pacing of the process can be modified, as can your word choices, to suit the mastery levels of your students. Scribing may be done in small groups for those students still needing help as the rest of your class begins to write independently. White board easels may be helpful for small group writing. They make it easy to add and delete ideas because they are so easy to erase. 🎭

Chapter 3
The Standing Ovation Checklists

Through doing enactments—and later, doing visualization, which you'll read about in Chapter 4: Encore Performances—students learn how to make connections to writing prompts so they can write more creative, detailed, personal responses. In short, enactments help improve the *content* of student writing. But to be more complete writers, students must also learn myriad other skills and techniques to present their ideas in the most effective way they can. The Standing Ovation Checklists help them learn and keep track of all their skills and techniques.

The Writing Puzzle

Students typically are taught one writing technique at a time, for example, punctuating dialogue or writing an effective hook. To display their skill with the given technique, they may be asked to write a paragraph or story using it, or they may simply be asked to identify the technique in isolated sentences. After they master each skill, a new skill is introduced and the process is repeated.

Do you see a disconnect here? When taught in isolation, writing skills are separate pieces of a puzzle that may or may not ever be put together.

Visualize the pieces of a child's puzzle strewn across a table. All the pieces are there, they just aren't connected. Some shapes are jagged, some are curved, and some are straight. Some may be upside down or backward. Worse yet, one or more of the pieces may have fallen on the floor, so the child doesn't even know they exist.

When students begin to connect the puzzle pieces, they will usually connect the straight edges first because these are the easiest to identify and set in place. Once all the straight edges are put together, the puzzle frame has been completed. It's connecting those pesky middle pieces that usually causes the most difficulty.

Like jigsaw puzzles, writing techniques may be separated into differently shaped pieces. Some, like those edge pieces, are easier to master. Others, like the middle pieces, are more difficult. And even if your students have all the pieces in front of them, they may not be sure how to connect them. Putting together the puzzle is a skill in itself and takes targeted practice. The Standing Ovation Checklists are tools to help your students connect the pieces of their writing puzzle.

The Completed Puzzle:
Writing for Assessments

For most writing occasions—during the school year and throughout students' lives—the selective use of a handful of appropriate writing techniques will produce an effective piece of writing. Not all elements are needed. For example, the use of dialogue may not always be appropriate. But writing for benchmark assessment tests, as we have discussed (pages 1–2), is a different genre of writing.

Here is one of the most important things to know about state assessment tests: they are scored not only on how creative, detailed, or original students' responses are, but also on the number of specific writing skills students demonstrate in their responses. Assessment scorers want to see completed puzzles with lots of pieces. They want to see a wide range of writing techniques. Students need to know that if they leave out even one tiny technique, their written responses may receive lower scores.

It's easy to know when you have used all the pieces in a jigsaw puzzle: there are no stray pieces, and the finished picture is an exact replica of the box top. When solving the writing puzzle, however, you can't manipulate physical pieces and you don't have a box top to reference as a guide. That's why solving the writing puzzle takes explicit, direct practice and should be started early in the school year. Many students will grasp the process quickly, but others will need much more time.

The skills described on the Standing Ovation Checklists are the skills looked for on most assessment scoring rubrics. We culled them from the scoring rubrics used for New Jersey and National Assessment of Educational Progress (the NAEP, or the "Nation's Report Card") tests, as well as from evaluators' written comments on scored tests in Texas, Massachusetts, California, and New Jersey. They are, beyond their existence on scoring rubrics, core writing skills that most middle-elementary students should be able to use.

The Standing Ovation Checklists:
An Overview

Since each prompt type requires a particular type of written response, we have created three distinct versions of the Standing Ovation Checklist. Each version of the list is aligned to one or two of the prompt types. The core of each list, though, is essentially the same. Most writing techniques are universal, while some may be appropriate for one kind of writing but not others. In addition, each Standing Ovation Checklist reproducible handout includes two blank checklist lines at the bottom for you to add any elements particular to your class or to the content you are covering at the time. These are optional.

The Standing Ovation Checklist for picture and speculative prompts serves as the foundation for all the lists. We discuss that list at length in this chapter. See chapters 10–12 for a discussion of how the lists for other prompts differ. You can also find reproducible handouts for all the checklists in their respective chapters. Here is the picture and speculative prompt list:

1. The story has a setting.
2. Characters in the story have names.
3. The beginning is a "hook" for the reader.
4. The characters in the story have a problem or conflict.
5. Dialogue, punctuated correctly, is included in the story.
6. At least two of the three forms of ending punctuation are included in the story: period (.), question mark (?), and exclamation point (!).
7. The story contains broad and accurate vocabulary.
8. The story includes action and rich details.
9. The story stays on the topic of the prompt.
10. The problem or conflict is resolved by the end of the story.
11. Each new paragraph is indented.
12. The story has been written neatly.
13. The title is related to the story.

1. The story has a setting

Ask your students to look critically at the picture prompt in order to identify location details. If there are setting details such as trees, a lake, or an ocean, students should take a cue from those details when describing the setting in their stories. If there is a blank background in the prompt, it is even more important for your students to create a specific location and describe it in their writing.

Look at the following samples, taken from real student essays:

> Lucy and Derrick decided to build their lemonade stand near the busy train station in town.

> Martin and Latiyah set up their lemonade stand in the park near the baseball diamond.

> Roberto and Francois sold their lemonade along the grassy curb outside the hospital.

2. Characters in the story have been assigned names

Your students should name the character(s) in the prompt. You might recommend that students pretend the characters have become their friends and each one needs to be named.

You may need to establish ground rules for the selection of names. Avoid the use of names of students in the class, as it may become a popularity contest, or it may be embarrassing for students. When scribing, you may want to have students nominate a few names, then have the group vote. The voting takes place with a hand signal while everyone's eyes are closed. That way students will not see how their friends are voting.

Some students may get antsy during the writing process. You may wish to build in movement opportunities for these students. "Physical Voting" is great for this. If a child suggests naming a character Harry, then a Harry vote could be cast by raising both arms straight up to make a capital H. If a choice is Pat, the signal could be patting oneself on the back.

3. The beginning is a "hook" for the reader

A hook is a beginning that will grab the reader's attention. Why is it important? A hook is what makes the reader excited about reading the rest of your student's text. In the case of writing for the test, if the hook engages the assessor's interest, your student is off to a positive start.

To emphasize the act of focusing on the characters in the prompt, ask your students to point to their own eyes and then to point to the characters in the picture. Ask what the first speaking character is going to say that would grab the assessor's interest. The dialogue can become part of the hook.

When connecting the checklist to the writing session, ask your students to look at the original picture prompt and to think about what the picture looked like when it was enacted by their classmates. Ask your students to think about the ideas generated during the prompt-enactment brainstorming session.

4. The characters in the story have a problem or conflict

Without a problem or conflict, your student's story will simply be a detailed setting. Characters need to be placed in a situation that allows them to identify their conflict and actively work to resolve it. Many conflict ideas come up during the brainstorming stage of the process.

Director's Note
Your students' writing is often a window to what they are dealing with in their real lives. Be alert for students who may be using these writing situations as a call for help. Should you suspect that a student is in crisis, immediately set up a conference with him or her. Your principal and guidance counselor also should be alerted to the situation. 🎭

Conflicts can usually be summed up in a sentence or two, as you can see from these writing samples:

Lucy and Derrick turned suddenly to see a dog running directly toward them.

Contrary to the morning weather report, the sky darkened and it started to rain as soon as Latiyah and Martin finished setting up their lemonade stand.

Roberto's mother called him home to get ready for his dentist appointment. What was Francois going to do now?

5. Dialogue, punctuated correctly, is included in the story

Have students look at the writing prompt and ask themselves the following question: if we could hear these characters talking right now, what would they be saying?

When you are scribing or working as a group, you may record answers on the chart paper. You might want to refer back to the scene the students enacted or even select two students, call them by the characters' names, and ask them to mime the scene again.

Direct your students to decide who is speaking first. It is always a good idea to ask students to explain their answers. This may give an insight into their thought process. Responses we've heard in our classrooms include:

"That boy's mouth is open wider, so he is speaking."

"She's leaning forward, so she's talking."

"His eyes are closed, so he's listening."

"That could be me and I know that I always speak first."

Director's Note

Assessors are looking for the student to demonstrate proficiency with a variety of writing skills, and dialogue is one item that can be effective and fun. But eager teachers and students must be careful to avoid "dialogue danger"—long exchanges of he-said-she-said dialogue. When overused, dialogue can clutter the response and cloud the focus of the story. When including dialogue in a writing response on a state assessment, it is the appropriate and careful use of quotation marks that will gain the better score. 🎭

6. At least two of three forms of ending punctuation are included in the story

These forms of punctuation include the period (.), the question mark (?), and the exclamation point (!). We often recommend that students open their story with a line of dialogue and end that first sentence with a question mark or an exclamation point. A powerful beginning, in which a student purposefully includes quotation marks, the name of the character, and a question mark or exclamation point, can grab the reader's attention and check off three elements from the checklist in one sentence.

Look at the samples below, taken from real student writing samples.

"Why don't we have any customers?" whined Lucy as she stood next to her best friend Derrick.

"Do you think there is something wrong with our lemonade?" asked Roberto as he watched Francois inspect the pitcher.

"Grab the cups!" screamed Latiyah as a gust of wind threatened to ruin Martin's lemonade display.

7. The story contains broad and accurate vocabulary

Good writing contains precise, descriptive words. This creates a more vivid reading experience for readers. For example, "Ruth went to school" does not create much of a mental image. Is she walking, riding on the bus, or something else? Is she late? Is it winter? Spring? Every sentence does not need to be crammed full of details, of course. We don't want students to exhaust their readers. But consider the previous sentence compared to the following one. With the addition of a precise verb and a couple of well-chosen details, the image becomes easy to picture:

Ruth pedaled her bike along the wet street toward school.

On tests, the use of evocative, accurate words shows the assessor that the writer has a strong vocabulary. Following are three activities you can work on with your students in order to help them expand their vocabularies and find more precise words to use in their writing.

Put *said* to bed

Said is a high-frequency sight word for many students. More specific speech tags can really evoke a voice in readers' minds. A visual activity called "Put *said* to bed!" can help students become aware of more speech tags and use them when appropriate. When reading aloud to your students, ask them to become "*said* detectives." While you are reading the story orally, your student detectives should listen for words that the author chose to use instead of the word *said*.

As you go through the story, you can list the words on a chart, or you can literally put the words on a bed graphic or outline you have drawn on the white board. As the synonyms are found, you or one of your students can print the word on the bed. Students may add their own synonyms also.

As a follow-up activity, ask students to collect *said* synonyms from stories or books they read on their own. They can keep these synonyms on a list or add them to a class word bank. The lists may be handy references when writing as a class or individually.

Nice was eaten by mice

Another overused word is *nice*. Students (and adults) may use it to describe a person, a place, an activity, the weather, and more. But just like *said*, the word *nice* is generic and doesn't provide readers with a very exact description.

Modify "Put *said* to bed" by calling it "*Nice* was eaten by mice!" and using the outline of mice as a visual aid. Your students must feed the mice with synonyms for *nice*. Again, the students become aware of alternatives for the high-frequency word through exposure to literature. Through a vocabulary-rich learning environment, they will come to recognize a variety of word choices to integrate into their writing pieces.

The 5 synonym switch

This is a useful editing activity that students can do on their own, in pairs, or in groups. When your students are finished writing their responses, ask them to reread their writing and underline five words that are not as strong or precise as they could be. These could be generic verbs such as *went* or *said*, or they might be nouns that need closer examination, such as *car* or *lunch*. Depending on the grade and skill-level of your students, you may need to provide plenty of support in helping them identify such words, or you may initially decide to require fewer words to be underlined and build up to five words.

Once students underline five words, have them erase one and replace it with a strong synonym. Then have them do it with the next underlined word, and so on until all the underlined words have been replaced. It's important to keep in mind that the point should be precision, not just using synonyms for the sake of using synonyms. The object is to use the *best* word. Again, some students may need more support than others in evaluating word choice. Tell students: If the first word you chose really was the right word, then don't switch it out for a synonym.

8. The story includes action and rich details

The purpose of enactments is to help students make personal connections to writing prompts, so they can bring their own experiences to their written responses. (See page 20 for more information about the different ways students may make personal connections to a text.) This personal experience is a source for actions and details that will bring to life the response for readers. When your students draw upon prior knowledge, they will be able to convey clear, lively ideas for their readers. Activating prior knowledge helps the writer visualize a story and it does the same for the reader.

Look for strong, active verbs in student writing—as well as details such as colors, emotions, tastes, textures, smells, and so on—as signs that they've made a connection. The use of adjectives and adverbs can also make a written piece more personal.

One way to help your students identify and use rich details is with the 5 MOPS strategy (page 24). If students keep this simple acronym in mind, they will remember to look for opportunities to use each of these techniques in their writing. However, make sure students know that they don't need to use every technique in every piece they write, and they should be careful not to force the use of any technique. If there is nothing for the character in a student's story to taste, for example, then adding a taste detail would be difficult and out of place.

Each part of the 5 MOPS strategy is a distinct writing skill that you may need to practice with your class. It's usually best to work on each strategy individually, because doing all of them at once could be overwhelming for students. As with the "Put *said* to bed" exercise, you may want to ask students to identify and list examples of the five senses, metaphor, onomatopoeia, personification, and simile in texts you read as a class and they read independently. These lists then become a resource for students to use in their writing, and you may also refer to them during scribing sessions.

9. The story stays on the topic of the prompt

While creativity in student writing is a wonderful quality, especially during free writing assignments, it is critical that students respond specifically to prompts when they are presented with them—especially when taking assessments. In these situations, there is a specific purpose for their writing. Students who write a story that takes tangents not related to the assignment or the prompt may receive an *OT* score: *Off Topic*. This results in the awarding of fewer points and possibly of no points.

Students demonstrate their ability to stay on topic when their written responses address the items in the bulleted directions for the particular task. For a picture prompt, that means writing a logical sequence of events that incorporates the moment in time displayed in the picture.

10. The problem or conflict is resolved by the end of the story

Tell your students: Don't leave your reader hanging! Students' stories need a beginning, where conflict is introduced; a middle, where it is developed as the characters try to resolve it; and an end in which the conflict is resolved—either negatively or positively. Once the writer has established the conflict, he or she takes the reader through a sensible sequence, with one event leading logically to another. Students gain an understanding of this process by reading and listening to examples of well-written stories and then adapting the style of those authors to their work.

Teachers can help students develop their ability to use this skill by modeling it during scribing exercises. Teachers do this by asking questions like, "What might happen after that? How might the characters try to fix their problem? What would happen if they succeed? What if they fail?" This discussion can help students imagine a logical sequence, building and resolving tension.

The following samples show conflicts resolving:

Their success was beyond their wildest dreams. The best friends had sold all of their lemonade, right down to the very last drop. Latiyah and Martin knew they would be able to make a difference in the lives of other children. That would make their guidance counselor really proud, too.

"We sure were lucky that the dog thought the mailman would be more fun to chase than us!" laughed Derrick.

"I can't wait to tell Mr. Marquez about this lemonade sale! If you weren't with me, I don't think he'd believe my story," laughed Roberto as he rode the bus to school with Francois the next morning.

Since your students most likely will not be writing fairy tales, their stories should not end with "The End" or "and they lived happily ever after." Help students understand how to craft stories that bring readers to a logical conclusion on their own. Such writing includes a solution to the problem or conflict, transitions words such as *finally* or *last,* and a feeling of closure in the tone or voice of the piece. Teachers may use examples of concluding paragraphs and even chapters of books to show students how authors write without using "The End."

As students gain more confidence and skill in writing, they may transfer their ability to develop and write a hook into the ability to leave a lasting impression on the reader. This is a skill that when applied enables the writer to take the reader full circle; the writer brings closure to the story for the reader.

Director's Note

Students must be very aware of the words "stop" and "end" on standardized tests. Make sure that prior to the test your students understand the important directions these words indicate. *Stop* means do not go any further in the booklet. Do not turn the page. *End* may mean the end of a particular section or the end of time for the students to work on a section. (Sometimes it is used as a synonym for *stop*.) Although *stop* and *end* may seem like common-sense direction words, it is important that students be reminded of how these words are used in standardized testing situations. 🎭

11. Each new paragraph is indented

Indenting a paragraph serves a variety of purposes for the writer and the reader. It signals the beginning of the story and transitions within the story. Paragraphs indicate a change of speakers in a conversation, a change in setting, a change in action, or a change in time. Finally, the indentation is a place keeper. It helps organize the story in the reader's mind.

When writing is composed on a computer, a blank line has become a common way to indicate a paragraph break. Since computers are rarely used during state assessments, students must be reminded to *always* indent a new paragraph—even when using a computer during the year. The skipping of lines between paragraphs is not suitable for hand-written assessment tasks.

12. The story has been written neatly

Students don't get extra points for this, but it sure makes their stories easier for the assessor to read. By the end of the year, you will have been deciphering your students' handwriting since early September and will probably have become somewhat of a mind-reader for a few students. Unfortunately, a psychic will not be evaluating your students' writing.

That's why legible handwriting must be enforced from the beginning of the year. Do not wait until late in the year to focus on handwriting. Do not accept the excuses of "Doctors have poor penmanship and they get away with it" or "I'll be using a computer to write everything at Harvard." Between September and May, do not accept work from students that is difficult to read. Demand that it be redone. Second chances are not given on state assessments!

During third grade, many students begin to learn cursive or script. Teachers often require their students to use it from that day forth. While cursive flows for some children, it doesn't for others. It is important in testing situations for the child to use whichever style of writing (cursive or print) is quickest, easiest, and neatest. Remind students to separate words with spaces and indent paragraphs. Additionally, steer them away from replacing dots with circles and hearts on top of the letters "j" and "i."

When test day arrives, make sure each child is equipped with sharpened pencils with good erasers. Since the test is timed, writers should have everything they need to work quickly.

A word about erasing: many students, especially gifted writers, will want to modify their ideas or change their ideas completely during the writing process. This is acceptable during a regular writing assignment—in fact it should be encouraged. During a state assessment, however, those same students might find themselves out of time after total or partial page erasure. You might wish to speak to your most creative thinkers about the situation, advising them to find an initial idea and stick with it when writing on state assessments. They must understand, however, that this is only during testing sessions and not at any other time. We do not want to demolish creativity during our quest for test scores.

If you have a student who has great difficulty with penmanship, it may be necessary for you to obtain an accommodation for that student. In the state of New Jersey, for example, students are able to have a scribe, a pencil grip, or other adjustments. These accommodations must be set up well in advance of the testing.

13. The title is related to the story

Every student's written response should have a title. Two qualities make a title strong: it accurately reflects what the piece is about, and it is interesting. When reading texts in class such as stories, poems, or books—or when students read independently—ask students to think about the titles these pieces have. Why do they think the author chose that title? What makes it interesting? Is it accurate? What other titles could the author have chosen? These questions help students focus on the art of titling. You can also have discussions about titling when scribing a response as a group. Ask for suggestions from the class, then discuss the accuracy and interest of each one, finally voting on which to use.

It's usually best if students add their titles when they're done writing. If the title is written first, it may reign in the creative process for some students. The title should fit the story; the story should not be created to fit the title. When scribing with your group, demonstrate this by coming up with the title after you've finished the story and read it out loud together. Some students, however, will want to use a title as a starting-off point for their writing. If individual students are more comfortable or confident creating a title first, by all means, allow them to continue. Ultimately, the point is not *when* you write the title but that it is a *quality* title, one that fits the story.

Using the Checklists

The Standing Ovation Checklists are flexible tools for teachers and students alike. You can use a list to guide enacting, group brainstorming, and scribing. Students can refer to it when drafting their written responses—to help them remember to include elements in their draft—and during revision. Knowing they can use a checklist as a guide and reference helps take out the mystery of writing, thus raising confidence and lowering anxiety. Checklists are also an important discussion point during student-teacher conferences.

When and how to use the checklist

When students take their assessments at the end of the year, they obviously cannot bring a checklist or any other reference material with them. The test measures what they know and can do on their own. Therefore, your students will need to *know* the information on the appropriate Standing Ovation Checklists when they take their assessments. A lot of information is on those lists, so it makes sense for you to introduce them to your students very early in the year.

The Standing Ovation Checklists are the teacher's friend. You can use a checklist to guide your students during brainstorming and improvisation. You might tape it to the back of an easel or keep it as a cue card. A checklist serves to keep the lesson on track, almost like a to-do list.

Because your students probably won't know all of the elements on the checklists on the first day of school, use the checklists as planning tools to see what your students know and what you need to teach throughout the months, weeks, and days leading up to the tests. If you're not sure if your students understand all the writing elements on the lists, you will want to spend some time teaching those elements. An afternoon spent coming up with examples of onomatopoeias can be valuable and fun.

Director's Note

If your students aren't familiar or comfortable with all the elements on the Standing Ovation Checklist you introduce, consider shortening the list to include only the elements you've worked on in class and adding elements back to the list as you cover them. Add elements back to the list quickly so it will be complete at least by midyear, giving students half of the school year or more to work with the complete checklist.

Another option is to post a blank checklist (just the title "Standing Ovation Checklist" and numbers down the left side) alongside an enlarged copy of the checklist as it appears in the book. The complete list serves as a map for the class. It's where they are going, their destination. Using a marker, fill in the blank list with the checklist items as you finish studying them in class. These two checklists may be used on a smaller scale for small group instruction or reproduced and put into a two-pocket folder (or glued to a manila file folder). 🎭

Another important way to use a checklist throughout the year is in coding student writing responses. After students write their drafts, have them go through them with a checklist as a reference, writing a small number in the draft that indicates where that item from the list is fulfilled. The coding shows you and your students what has been included in the written response and what, if anything, has been left out. Students can mark a list item each time it is used, but they don't have to. On page 37 is a sample student story coded using the picture prompt checklist (page 82).

Use a checklist or checklists consistently throughout the year, so your students begin to internalize them. By the end of the year, students should be comfortable enough to write without the lists as an aid (see pages 40–43).

Here are some ways you can use the Standing Ovation Checklists:

- **Make them into posters or project them on a screen.** Electronic versions of the checklists are available on the included CD-ROM. These can be printed at 200 percent on 17" x 22" paper (or larger—three cheers if you have access to a poster maker in your building!), made into a transparency, or projected directly from a computer. The advantage of a poster is that it is always up, but of course a projection can be larger and command more attention. You can also write on a transparency or type into the PDF while it's being projected, so these options are interactive. It can be helpful to refer to large versions of the checklists during brainstorming and scribing sessions, and they can be useful during individual writing time as well.

Example of a Coded Student Response

Lightning Saves the Day (13)

   (11) "Strike two!(6)" (5) yelled (7) the umpire as the ball flew into the catcher's brown mitt with a thud. (8) Upset at the call, the batter turned to look his father in the eye. Then he heard the catcher mutter under his breath, "Better luck next time, bro." The boys' dad felt that this was going to be his toughest game ever. His twin sons were playing against each other in the Little League championship game. (1) (3) (4)

   (11) Crack! (7) Suddenly the gray clouds opened up and hail the size of marbles started to hit the field. The air smelled like fresh rain, the grass was a green sponge, and then the fans started to run for cover (8). Looking to the outfield, Umpire Pat (2) stared at the scoreboard. The game was tied, his son Rob (2) was holding his favorite red aluminum bat and Ed (2) was holding the worn out catcher's mitt. Walking toward the other umpires, Pat avoided looking at his sons and their mother. She was running like a jackrabbit (7) (8) toward the family's red van.

   (11) With minutes passing by and people waiting for a decision about the game, Pat and the other umpires made the call. The game would be postponed until tomorrow at 3. Players from both teams started jumping in the puddles and sliding in the mud, forgetting that they were rivals. For a moment Pat wanted to join in, but he knew that Rob and Ed would be embarrassed and probably never speak to him again. With raindrops hanging off his cap, he walked toward his wife and the van.

   White lightning streaked across the black sky (7). Umpire Pat knew he had made the right decision. In a flash, Rob and Ed were in the back of the van. Mom looked worried. Pat wasn't sure what the boys would say. "Can we stop for pizza?(6)" the twins shouted(7). A loud sigh of relief bounced off the walls of the van as it rolled down the road toward the pizzeria. (10)

- **Provide hard copies for each student.** You may even want to laminate them and/or have students tape them to their desks or onto the cover of a binder or notebook. They may also, of course, simply keep a copy in their writing folders or somewhere readily accessible.

- **Provide electronic copies.** You might have students keep a copy on their flash drive or laptop if they have them. When students are writing on computers—especially if they're writing at home—it's important that they have a version of the list handy when they need it.

- **Require it as a cover sheet for each writing assignment.** This will help students remember to refer to the checklist when writing and editing. During individual conferences, ask your students to show you where each element is used in their stories.

- **Require it as a part of student writing binders, portfolios, or folders.** You could even record the number of elements each student includes on each assignment to track the students' progress throughout the year and assess their strengths and weaknesses. You could require that students plot their progress on a graph, tracking for themselves which elements they have mastered and which they need to work on.

For most teachers, the checklists will help take the subjectivity out of grading writing. Students know what is expected and will proceed accordingly when practicing their prompt responses. Parents can also use the checklists to help students when they're writing at home. This is another good reason to have electronic copies as well as hard copies available to students.

As the year progresses, your students will rely less and less on the lists as the elements become a natural part of their writing. They will become independent writers. Chapter 4: Encore Performances discusses this transition in depth.

Chapter 4
Encore Performances: Adjusting the Process Throughout the Year

As the school year progresses and you continue to use the prompt enactment process, your students will improve at turning writing prompts into written responses. Enacting will become more natural for them, ideas will flow more readily, and the writing techniques on the Standing Ovation Checklists will start to become second nature. As their skills and confidence increase, begin to transition them away from doing physical enactments and referring to physical checklists. Eventually, students should be able to *visualize* enactments, and they should *know* the writing techniques on the Standing Ovation Checklists without needing a physical list.

This is important for all writers, since they aren't likely to enact prompts and carry checklists for the rest of their writing lives. But it is especially important for those students, like yours, who will be taking a state assessment at the end of the year. They certainly won't have the opportunity (or time!) to enact writing prompts during the exam, and they aren't allowed to bring writing aids, such as a checklist, into the exam. That means, if you want your students to be prepared for the assessment, you are working with a deadline.

Adjusting Enactments and Writing Responsibility

The first time you do the enactment process with your class, you will enact a picture prompt and brainstorm and write a story together. We recommend you do this no matter what grade you teach. The resulting written response will have been produced by all of you. Over the next few weeks, repeat the process several times, decreasing the amount of group work and increasing the amount of individual work each time. The exact rate at which you make these changes will depend on the grade level and writing abilities of your class. (This is why early use of the enactment process is important.) No matter your students' grade level or skills, you should be incorporating their ideas into stories within the first month of school.

Early in the school year

Following is a general outline of how your first four to six weeks can progress. Use your knowledge about your students, as well as your schedule and your own strengths as a teacher, to adjust this progression to fit your needs. We recommend you do the process five times, with a different picture prompt each time.

1. Using the first picture, the students are involved in the enactment, participate in group discussion and analysis, and contribute story ideas. You scribe the beginning, middle, and end of the class story onto the chart paper or whiteboard.

2. Using the second picture, the students are involved in the enactment and discussion, and they contribute ideas. You scribe the majority of the beginning, middle, and end of the prompt response, but call upon a few students to write one or two words or sentences in the class story.

3. Using the third picture, the students are involved in the enactment and discussion, and they contribute ideas. You scribe the beginning and the middle of the story. Individually, students create their own endings.

4. Using the fourth picture, the students are involved in the enactment and discussion, and they contribute ideas. You scribe the beginning. Individually, students write the middle and the end on their own.

5. Using the fifth picture, the students are involved in the enactment, discuss it, contribute ideas, and write the beginning, middle, and end of their own complete stories. You are no longer the scribe.

Of course, even when the students are working individually, you are involved in the process. Walk among the students, look at their work, ask guiding questions, and provide support and praise as warranted by their work in progress.

The middle of the school year

Once your students have mastered the picture prompt enactment and writing process, it is time to move on to the genre (or genres) of prompt that appears on your state's assessment (if it's not a picture prompt). Start by reading the chapter in Part 3 of this book that corresponds with that prompt type. You will want to work with your students on each type of writing that is required (for example persuasive writing). You'll also need to help them figure out what to enact when the prompt is not simply a picture for them to look at and re-create. Finally, highlight specific details of the Standing Ovation Checklist that are different in the new prompt compared to the picture prompt. All of this information is discussed in the Part 3 chapters.

During this time, continue doing enactments as a class or in groups. Your goal is to get students as comfortable and skilled as possible with the process of looking at a writing prompt, figuring out how to enact it, analyzing the enactment, and writing a response that includes a personal connection for them. This is a good time to look for opportunities to differentiate, as you will likely see students begin to separate into different skill levels. Some students will be strong at certain parts of the process and weaker at others. Flexible grouping can be especially helpful at this time. See pages 55–56 for more on differentiation.

Later in the school year

Soon after winter break, it is time to begin teaching your students to visualize enactments rather than actually do them. You might introduce this transition by looking at a prompt together as a group and discussing the different ways someone *could* enact it. Then tell your students to close their eyes and create a movie in their minds. They can imagine one of the ideas the class brainstormed, or they can imagine their own ideas. Say, "How would you enact this prompt if you were able to get up and do it?"

Help students by asking them to remember enactments they've done earlier in the year. Remind them, too, that the goal of the enactment or visualization is to help them make a personal connection to the prompt. What does the prompt remind them of from their own experiences? Urge them to imagine lots of details in their visualized enactment. These details will be useful in their writing.

Just as they do with enactments, students next analyze their visualization, probing it for ideas to write about. Although eventually they will need to do this mentally (and silently), when you are introducing visualization encourage them to describe what they see in their mind. When reflecting upon their mental imagery, students should ask themselves questions similar to the ones you asked during group discussion. Again, for the first few times your students do visualizations, you may orally provide some general discussion questions for them to think about. Take a look at the discussion question suggestions in the Part 3 chapters for inspiration.

You may continue with this group approach to visualization and analysis for a short while, but you'll want to have students visualizing on their own before too long—without the aid of a class discussion. After a few weeks of visualization, students should be able to take a writing prompt, visualize an enactment, mentally analyze it, and write a response, all on their own.

This period of transition is another good time to differentiate. Carefully observe the progress and needs of your students. Those displaying the ability to visualize and write early on should have the opportunity to advance at their own pace. Those who need additional support and modeling may meet in small groups for more direct instruction.

Adjusting the Role of the Standing Ovation Checklist

All students need to be able to write without the list by the time they take their assessment at the end of the school year. The time to *start* weaning students from the physical checklists is soon after winter break, the same time you're teaching them to visualize enactments. This timing is important, partly for emotional reasons: some of your students may feel they are not ready to give up the security of the checklists. If you get them used to it early on, they will have more time to gain confidence in writing without it. Positive reinforcement and praise go a long way during this time.

For many students, applying the checklists to their writing evolves easily into habit, just from practicing it enough times. The skills on the lists become second nature to them. Some students may need a little nudge and some additional support, but they too will soon be writing confidently without the checklist. Other students may have difficulty with this step. For these students, you'll need to provide plenty of scaffolding and other differentiation techniques. By January, you will likely have a good idea of which students need what, and you can differentiate accordingly.

Start the weaning process by removing the personal copies from those students who no longer need the visual reminder. These are students who you notice are not using the checklist when they write. They have internalized the checklist. These may be students who can close their eyes and visualize the checklist in their mind or students who have used it so often that it's become a habit. If you recognize such students even before January, by all means encourage them to stop using the checklist sooner. You can leave any wall copies you have posted for a bit longer, but those, too, should be removed soon.

Over the next few weeks, work closely with students who still rely on the list. Help them internalize the list or visualize it just as they do enactments. We encourage you to support students' mastery of the elements on the lists rather than drilling or quizzing them on the lists themselves.

- Success can occur through continued practice that is broken down into manageable sections. Work with the student to write a beginning and have the child self-evaluate what was included in that portion. Praise the child's success, and work with the student to include the missing elements. Then, repeat a few more times with different prompts until the child's performance has improved. Next, add the middle and then the end. Such gradual buildup and reinforcement for approximations and success may be what this student needed to internalize and demonstrate mastery of this genre of writing.

- Another idea is to give students a blank checklist and a written response. The students read the written response and, as they recognize a checklist element, write it on the chart. The written response acts as a prompt for the student to remember the elements. We have worked with teachers who color code the checklist. While the student does not have to go through the elements in a sequential lockstep manner while writing, there are certain elements that fit the beginning and others that clearly fit the conclusion. Teachers use highlighters to indicate those for the students.

- Games are another strategy that may work for memorization. Concentration, bingo, and Jeopardy! are popular options. You can also find Standing Ovation Checklist Playing Cards on pages 47–52. Many games can be made from these. And, although drill-and-skill is not right for all students, some do learn best this way.

Customizable versions of Jeopardy! are available on the Internet (techteachers.com/jeopardytemplates.htm is a good source). You can project the game using your computer. The use of this game for preparation can also be a collaborative effort between classes and teachers. Share what you create and work with your colleagues to trade successful tools.

Eventually, and no later than one month prior to the exam, no student should have personal copies of the checklist. Waiting too long to have students work without the checklists may cause anxiety and trepidation, which can impede a student who might otherwise perform well on the test.

Once checklists are removed, make checklist-free writing into a challenge or game. Students write prompt responses, self-evaluate their writing against a checklist to see how many elements they included, record the total number of elements they included, and then try to beat their total the next time. Have students create a bar graph or line graph to chart their progress. You can use these graphs as data to plan instructional groups or to help you see which students may need additional help or a different approach.

Group writing can be beneficial during this time, too. Put students into groups of four or five, give them a prompt, and ask them to write a group response. This allows students with different strengths to teach each other. (See pages 58–59 for more on kids teaching kids.) It can be a lot of fun, too.

The Standing Ovation Checklist Playing Cards

The Standing Ovation Checklist Playing Cards on pages 47–52 are another fun tool you can use to help students memorize the checklists and get comfortable writing without them. Each deck of cards corresponds to one of the writing prompt types and includes two blank cards for you to add customized content. Copy the cards (or print them from the CD-ROM), perhaps onto colored paper or cardstock for durability, and cut them out. For even more durability, laminate them. You could also print the cards out at 200 percent onto 17″ x 22″ paper to make enlarged cards for full class or group work.

The cards are a flexible tool. You can use them in class work, group work, and individual writing assignments. You can use them as a resource at a writing station. Students with visual/spatial and kinesthetic strengths may find manipulating cards helpful in learning the techniques. Your most capable students might enjoy the challenge of creating a game to play with the cards.

Following are a few specific suggestions for using the cards. Feel free to adapt these to your needs or make up your own.

Writer of the week

Hand out one or more cards to each student in your class, making sure that each element from the list is represented at least once. (Depending on the size of your class, you may give one card to two or three students to share.) Have students place their cards faceup on their desks.

Ask for a student volunteer to share his or her story. You might plan this beforehand, so you can make copies of the story for everyone. You might take spontaneous volunteers and use a document camera or opaque projector to enlarge the story onto a screen, as well, so it's easier to code the piece as a group (see page 57). Have the writer read the story out loud while everyone else follows along silently. This supports reading comprehension, as students will be able to hear the story as they read. As students listen and read along, they should take careful notice to see if the element on their card is included correctly in the story. As soon as a specific element is used, students turn the checklist card facedown.

When the student writer finishes reading his or her story, members of the student audience give an enthusiastic round of applause. Next, ask the students to look around the table or classroom to see which cards are still faceup. These are the elements that they could not locate in the written piece. Review the story as a group to verify that indeed those strategies are missing.

Award the student writer one point for each element included in the story. We never subtract points for items not included in the written response. You may keep track of points on a chart or graph in the classroom. The student with the most points at the end of one week is considered "Writer of the Week." This student becomes the class writing-expert for the next few days, acting as an assistant for other writers in the class.

The "Writer of the Week" title rotates among the students; no one owns the title week after week. You can ensure this by selecting two new writers each week to compete. You may ask for volunteers or simply choose different students each week to share their stories with the class. If you have a tie, it's fine to have a pair of winners. You act as a monitor and make allowances so that students take turns acting as writing assistants.

The purpose of writer of the week is for students to see each other as possible sources of information, to develop a sense of community in the classroom, and to develop students' confidence and leadership skills. The writer of the week does not grade or officially evaluate the work of other students. His or her role is peer guidance and support. You know your students and the dynamics of your class, so if you need to set up different (stricter) guidelines for this activity, for example to curtail bossiness, by all means do so. You want this to be positive for you and the students.

Left is right!

Prepare enough Standing Ovation Checklist Playing Cards for each student in your class to have a full deck. (With so many decks needed, this would be a great opportunity to invite parents or students to help with the copying and cutting of the cards.) Have students place all their cards along the right side of their desks. As they include an element from the checklist in their stories, they move that card to the left side of the desk. Once all cards have been moved to the left side, a student visually sees that his or her writing contains all necessary elements.

Writing relay

Present a picture prompt to the class and distribute checklist cards to students. Place chart paper and markers at the front of your room and invite a student holding card number one to the chart paper to write a sentence that employs element number one. When that student is finished, call up a student with card number two and ask that student to write a sentence that employs the element on that card—but this sentence must continue the story begun by the first student. Continue calling students to the front to contribute a sentence to the story, with the last student finishing the story. When the story is finished, have the class read it out loud and give themselves a round of applause.

Director's Note

You may want to reorder the cards to make them work best for your class. For example, start with card number 3, "The story has a hook," and put setting and character names later. Also, if an element has already been covered, a student holding that element card should use it again. For example, dialogue may be included in a hook that was already written, but a student with the dialogue card may write more dialogue. In addition, you may want to remove card number 11, "Each new paragraph is indented," and card number 12, "The story has been written neatly," and save them for the self-editing period at the end. 🎭

You may also do two or three simultaneous writing relays using teams. In this case, you can award a point to the first team that successfully writes a sentence using each element. In the team version, you may randomly select cards or go in order. The team with the most points when you have gone through all cards is the winner.

Adjusting to Authentic Test Prompts

As the test draws near, you can help students prepare even more by exposing them to authentic writing prompts that have appeared on recent exams in your state. Many states make the questions from the previous year's test available at their department of education's Web site. Other states may provide samples if requested via their Web site. If you cannot find genuine samples from your state's test, representative samples are available at www.educationworld.com and other Web sites. You will also find several examples of authentic prompts on pages 44–45.

When you assign these writing prompts to your students, make sure they know that they actually appeared on previous state assessments. Ask them to notice how each prompt is written and set up. Are they sure they understand the directions? Are they sure they know exactly what is expected of them? Are there bullet points that must be answered? It makes no difference how well your students are able to write if their responses are not direct responses to the prompt. Remind your students how important it is to read the directions carefully in order to find out exactly what is expected from them during the writing assessment.

Following are samples of authentic test prompts from various states.* Remember, each state determines which prompts are included in their assessments, and at which grade level they will be addressed, so these samples may not be representative of your state. Also, each state may use different terminology when describing the prompt.

Picture prompt samples

These examples show typical questions on picture prompts. Search at www.state.nj.us/education/assessment to see the pictures provided.

1. Using the picture as a guide, write a story about what might be happening.
   (New Jersey, grade 3)
2. A picture can tell a story, but different people will see different stories in the same picture. Look at this picture. What story do you think it tells? Write what you think is happening in this picture. What is the story behind it?
   (New Jersey, grade 5)

Speculative prompt samples

Some states refer to these as narrative prompts.

1. One morning you wake up and discover that you are only six inches tall. Write a story about what happens next.
   (North Carolina, grade 4)
2. Think about a special person in your life. This person may or may not live with you.
   - Write a story about one day you spent with this special person.
   (Georgia, grade 5)

3. Write a composition about a time when something surprising happened.
   (Texas, grade 4)
4. Write a composition about a time when you thought you were right.
   (Texas, grade 7)

Persuasive prompt samples

1. Your teacher wants your class to choose the next field trip. You can go anywhere in the world for as long as you would like. Where would you like to go?
   - Write a speech to convince your class and teacher that your field trip is the one to take. Include specific details to explain why your field trip would be the best.
   (Georgia, grade 5)
2. A school committee is creating a mural (wall painting) that will feature students' favorite book or movie characters. Only a limited number of characters can be included. Each student has been asked to nominate a character from a book or a movie.
   - Select a character to be featured as part of the mural and write a letter to the school committee justifying your selection.
   (North Carolina, grade 7)
3. Your principal would like to add a new class that is not currently offered in your school. The principal has asked students to make recommendations about new classes. Decide what class you would recommend for your school.
   - **Directions for Writing**
     Write a letter to convince the principal that your new class is the best one for the school. Be sure to include detailed reasons.
   (Georgia, grade 8)
4. Take a position on whether violent shows should be shown on television. State your position and explain why you

---

* These prompts originally appeared on state assessments in New Jersey, North Carolina, Georgia, Texas, and Oregon.

think violent shows should or should not be shown on television.

(North Carolina, grade 7)

Poetry prompt samples

Some states call these explanatory prompts.

1. (Students first listen to and read the Shel Silverstein poem "Moon-Catchin' Net.") Has there ever been something you wanted very much that you may or may not have been able to get? Write about what you wanted. Include the following:

   - What did you want to have and why did you want this?

   - If you got it, explain how it happened and why you were successful.

   - If you didn't get it, explain why not.

   - Explain how you might be successful in getting it in the future.
   (New Jersey, grades 3–5)

2. In "The Horn I Scorn," the poet Jill Esbaum writes about a problem that comes from having to share. At one time or another, most of us have to share something with someone else. Write a composition about the difficulties of having to share something you value.

   In your composition, be sure to

   - Describe what it is you have to share

   - Discuss the problems that come from having to share it

   - Explain how you solved the problems
   (New Jersey, grade 4)

Quote or adage prompt samples

Some states call these explanatory prompts.

1. You are submitting an essay to the annual essay competition at your school. You have been asked to consider how the following quotation is related to you.

   "You make the world a better place by making yourself a better person."
   —Scott Sorrell

   Write an essay explaining what this quotation means to you. Use details and examples in your essay.
   (New Jersey, grade 6)

2. Walt Disney once said, "If you can dream it, you can do it." Tell a story about a time when this was true for you or someone you know.
   (Oregon, grades 6–8)

3. As part of a language arts class assignment, you have been asked to consider the following quotation:

   "The function of education is to teach one to think critically. Intelligence plus character—that is the goal of true education."
   —Martin Luther King Jr. (1929–1968)

   Write an essay in which you explain whether you agree or disagree with this quotation. You may use one or more examples from your experiences. Be sure to use details, reasons, and examples in your explanation
   (New Jersey, grade 8)

Test Day Preparation Tips

Having given tests, taken tests, and prepared students for tests, we know that test anxiety knows no age boundary. Once your students are able to visualize both the enactment process and the use of the checklist, it is time for some additional test preparation.

One of the key factors is timing. Do not take for granted that your students understand how much time they have on the assessments. Ask how many of your students think they know what a minute feels like. How about five minutes? Twenty minutes?

Ask them to stand silently next to their desks. Cover up the classroom clock and instruct your students to stand on one leg for one minute and sit down when they think the minute is up. You may be surprised how many of your students do not understand how much time one minute actually is—let alone two minutes, or ten, or forty! How can we expect our students to write within a specific amount of time if they have no idea how long that time is? Since being timed on the test adds pressure to an already stressful situation, knowing how to estimate what time they actually have can help students manage the process.

Time may be a huge issue for some students with learning differences, including your gifted and talented students. Often, students (especially your most creative students) spend a lot of time collecting their ideas. This would be fine if their idea-collection was done during everyday classroom writing rather than assessment writing. During assessments, however, many of your best writers may not have time to write their ideas because they spent too much time percolating them.

Similarly, many students, especially your perfectionists, may begin writing and decide halfway through that they could do a better job and start over. After wasting a huge amount of precious time, and creating eraser-ravaged test booklets, these writers will have little or no time left to start over. Teach your students that once they begin writing on an assessment, they should not start over. There simply isn't time.

If you begin timing many things in your classroom early in the year (math skills, reading passages, etc.) and making it fun, you may help your students understand and respect the timing issue, and not be frightened or overwhelmed by it. In addition, begin timing their written responses in class well ahead of the testing date—perhaps as early as January.

Other tips

- By January, you should have checked student files to ascertain if any of your students have a document that contains required test taking accommodations.

- Other than covering or removing items such as the Standing Ovation Checklists, don't make any drastic changes in the classroom environment on test day. There is comfort in the familiar.

- Make sure students know what to expect on test day, and what your role will be. You don't want to add anxiety, or seem like the "bad guy" when you are not allowed to help them during the test. They must know you are there with them, but you are not allowed to help them write.

- Look at your clock to make sure it works; get a watch and set it to the official time.

- Have plenty of sharpened pencils on hand with good erasers.

- Send a note home to parents and guardians informing them about the test dates and requesting that they become part of the test-taking team by helping their students get a good night's rest and eat a healthy breakfast before the test.

Once the test is over, encourage students to give themselves a round of applause for a job well done. Give yourself a silent pat on the back, too. While your stomach may be doing flip-flops and gray hairs may be sprouting, keep in mind the students see themselves through your eyes. Never let them see you sweat!

Standing Ovation Checklist Playing Cards

1. The story has a setting.

For picture and speculative prompts

2. Characters in the story have names.

For picture and speculative prompts

3. The beginning is a "hook" for the reader.

For picture and speculative prompts

4. The characters in the story have a problem or conflict.

For picture and speculative prompts

5. Dialogue, punctuated correctly, is included in the story.

For picture and speculative prompts

6. At least two of the three forms of ending punctuation are included in the story: period (.), question mark (?), and exclamation point (!).

For picture and speculative prompts

Standing Ovation Checklist Playing Cards (continued)

7. The story contains broad and accurate vocabulary.

For picture and speculative prompts

8. The story includes action and rich details.

For picture and speculative prompts

9. The story stays on the topic of the prompt.

For picture and speculative prompts

10. The problem or conflict is resolved by the end of the story.

For picture and speculative prompts

11. Each new paragraph is indented.

For picture and speculative prompts

12. The story has been written neatly.

For picture and speculative prompts

13. The title is related to the story.

For picture and speculative prompts

14. _____

For picture and speculative prompts

15. _____

For picture and speculative prompts

Standing Ovation Checklist Playing Cards (continued)

1. The response uses the format of a letter (header, date, greeting, closing).

For persuasive prompts

2. The response is written to the audience described in the prompt.

For persuasive prompts

3. The opening includes a hook, a statement of your position, and a summary of your supporting reasons.

For persuasive prompts

4. The response includes at least three persuasive reasons to support your position.

For persuasive prompts

5. Each reason is supported by details.

For persuasive prompts

6. The reasons are addressed in the same order as presented in the opening.

For persuasive prompts

7. The response includes at least three transitional words.

For persuasive prompts

8. The response acknowledges another point of view in one or two sentences.

For persuasive prompts

9. The closing makes a plea to the reader to agree with you.

For persuasive prompts

Standing Ovation Checklist Playing Cards (continued)

10. At least two of the three forms of ending punctuation are included in the response: period (.), question mark (?), and exclamation point (!).

For persuasive prompts

11. The response contains broad and accurate vocabulary.

For persuasive prompts

12. The response includes action and rich details.

For persuasive prompts

13. The response stays on the topic of the prompt.

For persuasive prompts

14. Each new paragraph is indented.

For persuasive prompts

15. The response has been written neatly.

For persuasive prompts

16. _____

_____
_____
_____
_____
_____
_____

For persuasive prompts

17. _____

_____
_____
_____
_____
_____
_____

For persuasive prompts

18. _____

_____
_____
_____
_____
_____
_____

For persuasive prompts

Standing Ovation Checklist Playing Cards (continued)

1. The opening includes a hook, the title of the poem, quote, or adage, and the author's name.

For poetry and quote or adage prompts

2. The response draws a connection between the text's main idea and the writer's personal experience.

For poetry and quote or adage prompts

3. The response includes least two of the three forms of ending punctuation: period (.), question mark (?), and exclamation point (!).

For poetry and quote or adage prompts

4. The response contains broad and accurate vocabulary.

For poetry and quote or adage prompts

5. The response includes action and rich details.

For poetry and quote or adage prompts

6. The response is written in a logical sequence and uses transitional words.

For poetry and quote or adage prompts

7. Key ideas are developed with details and direct connections to the text.

For poetry and quote or adage prompts

8. The response is written for an audience who does not know the writer.

For poetry and quote or adage prompts

9. The response concludes with a strong ending.

For poetry and quote or adage prompts

Standing Ovation Checklist Playing Cards (continued)

10. The response uses proper grammar and word usage.

For poetry and quote
or adage prompts

11. The response stays on the topic of the prompt.

For poetry and quote
or adage prompts

12. Each new paragraph is indented.

For poetry and quote
or adage prompts

13. The response has been written neatly.

For poetry and quote
or adage prompts

14. _____
_____
_____
_____
_____
_____
_____

For poetry and quote
or adage prompts

15. _____
_____
_____
_____
_____
_____
_____

For poetry and quote
or adage prompts

Part 2

Extending and
Optimizing the Process

Chapter 5
Differentiating the Enactment Process

Differentiated instruction is teaching that accounts for the fact that students are not all the same. They have varying background knowledge, readiness, language, interests, and preferences in learning, and as such they cannot be expected to learn in the same ways. To differentiate instruction, we teach in ways that take advantage of each student's unique strengths and support each student's weaknesses. We also allow students to demonstrate their learning based upon their specific learning preferences. In short, differentiation means adapting instruction to meet individual needs.

Connecting Students' Natural Strengths to Their Writing

The enactment process—which includes interpreting prompts, enacting them, and writing responses—provides many natural opportunities to differentiate instruction. It allows you to satisfy language arts standards while acknowledging the unique learning styles of all students. The whole point of enactments is to urge students to connect the writing task to their own lives. When students write about something they are connected to, they are almost by definition taking advantage of their strengths. Their final product—a written response—will reflect their unique experiences.

Enactments are flexible. They may be done in a variety of ways, including nonverbally. Students may contribute actively, enthusiastically, or subtly. They may work alone or in groups. Artistically inclined students may design sets, verbally strong students may write dialogue, gregarious students may use humor,

and imaginative students may add unique, creative detail to their stories. Some students may sing and dance. Writing responses, too, is a task that's inherently flexible, because students are encouraged to write to their own strengths.

You can differentiate instruction by content, process, and product.

- **Content** is what students need to know and be able to do. In the case of this book, the goal is that they be able to make personal connections with writing prompts and write creative, personal, skillful responses.

- **Process** refers to the activities students do as they engage with the content. The enactment process itself can be differentiated at every step.

- **Product** means the ways students show what they've learned. In this case, the product is their written work.

In this chapter, you'll find specific techniques for differentiating—techniques that provide support and flexibility—in these areas. You'll find that some techniques can be used naturally in more than one of the areas.

Differentiating Content

Scaffolding

Scaffolding means providing direct support for the varying needs of the students in your classroom. There are several ways to do this. As you work through the enactment process for the first time with your students, you are scaffolding for the whole class (see chapter 2). You and your class will do every step of the process together—enacting a prompt, analyzing the enactment by discussing it, and writing an appropriate prompt response.

Scaffolding enactments

- Model an enactment yourself, either alone or as part of a group.
- Scaffold for shy, nervous, or struggling students by providing lots of specific direction, right down to suggestions on where to stand and what to say or do. You can also allow them to simply re-create a prompt without adding dialogue or movement. Again, offering to join a group to enact with them can take some pressure off.
- Allow shy, struggling, or nervous kids to watch others model enactments first. This will give them the chance to gain confidence prior to taking the stage.

Scaffolding writing responses

- Early in the year, provide a copy of the Standing Ovation Checklist for every student to keep on his or her desk or elsewhere so students can refer to it while writing.

- Use the Standing Ovation Card Deck to provide different ways for students to engage with the Standing Ovation Checklists. (See pages 47–52.)
- Meet with students individually to discuss their drafts.
- Provide time in class for students to work on elements on the Standing Ovation Checklists in writing situations not associated with enactments.

Flexible grouping

Working in groups is not a built-in part of the enactment process, but can be a valuable way to differentiate both enacting and writing. The key word to this type of grouping is "flexible." Sometimes it may be beneficial to group students according to ability or skill level, other times according to interest or talent area, and other times you may simply allow students to choose the group they would like to work with socially. Since all students have strengths, working in groups allows them to teach and learn from each other in an active way.

Flexible grouping for enactments

- Grouping by interest or talent can be a fun way for students to explore personal connections to prompts from many different angles. Give interest groups different assignments, with the whole class working toward producing one big enactment. For example, group those students with strong artistic interest and/or abilities together to create scenery and props for the enactment. Those students with strong music abilities may work together to create background music, sound effects, or even a theme song. Another group—verbally strong students—might write dialogue, and another group might be actors. The process will promote teambuilding within each group and as a class.

- As students develop individual strengths and competencies, you may group them according to ability and willingness to enact prompts. Stronger, more comfortable enactors may work together, further building on their strengths as they encourage and teach each other. Those students needing more guidance from you—and fellow classmates—may work together. Provide all groups with the same prompt and have each group present its enactment at the end of the period. Students will see firsthand that there is no right or wrong way to do an enactment. The celebrated difference is based upon individual interpretation and creativity.

Flexible grouping for writing

- After students have written a few essays and worked with a Standing Ovation Checklist, it is easy to group them according to their strengths and weaknesses on the list. For example, one group may consist of students needing help with different forms of punctuation, while another group may consist of students needing direct instruction on writing dialogue. Due to the flexible nature of this type of grouping, students can work in different groups on different skills throughout the year.

- After your students have written responses for picture, speculative, persuasive, quote or adage, and poetry prompts, you can group them by response type. Display a picture prompt for all to see and assign a different response type to each group. (You might group students according to writing ability, interest, strength or weakness toward a type of response.) Assign one group to write a story response to the picture and another group to write a speculative response telling what happened before or after the picture. Give other groups a quote, adage, poem, or persuasive prompt that is aligned to the picture. Each group will write and share its response. Students will learn from the different skills and personalities in their group, and they'll understand how all writing is related and that the skills required to write a speculative response are similar to the skills required to write a persuasive or poetry response.

Differentiating Process

Cubing

Cubing is a reading and writing differentiation technique that helps students think about a subject from six different angles, using the following verbs to initiate the thought process:

- describe
- compare
- associate
- apply
- analyze
- argue

Looking at a single subject (such as a writing prompt) from these six perspectives can help students develop critical and creative thinking skills. They are forced to look at writing prompts in new ways. They may see that exciting stories are multidimensional, and, like real life, filled with twists and turns. The more twists and turns our students are able to include in their responses, the more interesting their written work will be—which results in better test scores. You may assign students to work alone, in pairs, in groups, or as a class on enactments or written responses using the different perspectives.

Director's Note

You may simply assign the six perspectives, or you may use an actual cube and have students roll it to see from which perspective they are to write. If you choose to use actual cubes, you can purchase wooden cubes at a hardware store, make cubes from construction paper, or simply use a single game board die.

Cubing the enactment

When students use cubing perspectives to guide their enactments, they are forced to think outside the box. This works if you are using cubing's traditional six verbs, but it can be interesting and productive to modify the perspectives. For example, if one perspective says, "It begins to rain halfway through the enactment," students are forced to stop, rethink the prompt, and refocus their enactment. It can change their storylines completely. You can roll the die once before the enactment, then roll it again partway through, making them change course. Exciting, unexpected details can add value to a written response. Cubing is a great way to open the door to students' creativity.

At the top of the next column is a sample set of enactment modifiers for cubing. Feel free to make up your own or to ask your students to create them.

If the student rolls:	The student's enactment motivator will be:
1	It begins to rain halfway through the enactment.
2	A nonspeaking clown must be included in the enactment.
3	One of the characters must exit during the enactment.
4	The enactment must be humorous.
5	The enactment must include audience participation.
6	The enactment must take place in the future.

Cubing written responses

Cubing for the writing half of the enactment process is similar to cubing enactments. As with cubing enactments, you can use cubing's traditional six verbs, but modifying the perspectives also can be interesting. Have students write from another person's point of view, such as in the following table.

If the student rolls:	The student's writing response perspective will be:
1	Write from the perspective of the main character.
2	Write from the perspective of a young child.
3	Write from the perspective of your teacher.
4	Write from the perspective of someone who is invisible.
5	Write from the perspective of a famous person.
6	Write from the perspective of a supporting character.

As before, we encourage you to make up your own perspectives or to ask your students to make them up. Giving students ownership over the assignment can increase their investment in the work. And as they examine a writing occasion from different points of view, they learn to step out of their own shoes and slip into someone else's to find rich details that they otherwise may have ignored.

Looking through another person's eyes can also help students become more sensitive to those around them. This can be especially valuable when students are asked to respond to persuasive prompts. Ask students to argue multiple sides of the same issue.

Director's Note

This idea works for teachers, too, and might be worth a try with your staff. We ask teachers to bring the same baseball picture prompt to life during each workshop we present. One particularly enthusiastic group of language arts teachers achieved a collective "Aha" moment during their baseball enactment. The teacher playing the role of the catcher said that when she knelt down and became the catcher, she saw the game in a whole new way. She pitches in a summer woman's softball league and had never thought about the game from the catcher's point of view until that day. (She also said she's glad she's not a catcher!)

Each teacher played the role of the catcher to see what she meant. Besides complaining that their knees hurt and that it was difficult to keep their balance, teachers experienced the impact of a speeding ball crossing the plate, aiming right for them. Writing their story from the perspective of the catcher was very different from writing it from the perspective of the pitcher. Their stories were filled with wonderful new vocabulary and rich, vivid details about their feelings and attitudes toward their new position.

They were so excited about learning this new perspective that they recommended for the next prompt they write about state assessments from the perspective of one of their students. Now wouldn't that be interesting? 🎭

The more often you cube, the more uses you will find for it. Even simply rolling a die can add excitement, anticipation, and chance to your classroom. Students may even feel like they are playing while learning, turning what could have been a boring writing assignment into an enjoyable one.

Kids teaching kids

Kids teaching kids is a powerful tool for differentiation because of the way it helps students retain information. Research shows that students retain far more of new learning when they are given the opportunity to teach others or to immediately use their learning. Happily, kids teaching kids is built into the enactment process by virtue of the fact your class will work together enacting and scribing. You can also create more kids teaching kids opportunities in the following ways.

Kids teaching kids during enactments

Early in your school year, you will notice students in your class who display strong enactment abilities. As they hone their craft in the areas of acting, dance and movement, or writing, allow these students to take on the roles of enactment experts by becoming the director, choreographer, or scriptwriter of an enactment. These students can guide their fellow classmates in how the enactment could be acted out, how movement could be included, and how the enactment could be captured in written form. The director and choreographer may wish to role-play their vision of the enactment, while the scriptwriter may guide the class discussion of the enactment to include the elements on the Standing Ovation Checklist.

Kids teaching kids during writing responses

- Have students edit each other's writing responses using the Standing Ovation Checklist. They should code the response with numbers showing where each item on the list is completed. (See page 37 for a sample coded response.) Once the coding has been completed, have students meet in pairs to discuss their writing. This dialogue between students is important because students explore the reasons behind their writing and editing decisions.

- The Writer of the Week activity is another great kids teaching kids opportunity. See page 42.

Tiered assignments

Tiered assignments are structured to meet the varied needs and mastery levels of students in your class by providing more than one way for students to reach the same basic learning goals. The assignment is divided into levels, or tiers, of challenge or complexity. A typical tiered assignment will have three levels: for struggling students, on-target students, and advanced students. You will need to use the information you've learned about your students (see pages 11–16) as well as any additional pre-assessment you've done to establish the readiness of each student. All assignments should be rigorous and similar, and the learning goals of each should be the same.

A good time to use tiered assignments is when you begin to wean your students from using the physical copy of the Standing Ovation Checklist (see pages 40–43). The following chart shows one way an assignment may be tiered. For this lesson, the class has been given a prompt and completed a prompt enactment. Students now will write their responses without the checklist.

Tier 1 (Struggling Writers) Students use the Standing Ovation Playing Card Deck (see pages 47–52) to aid them.	Instruct students to place all cards along the right side of their desks. As they include an element from the checklist in their response, they move the card to the left side of their desks. Once all cards have been moved to the left side, they will visually see that their writing contains all necessary elements.
Tier 2 (On-Target Writers) Students make "checklist-free" writing into a chart game.	Students write their prompt response without the Standing Ovation Checklist. Upon completion, they look at the checklist for two minutes. Then they get to revise without the list in front of them.
Tier 3 (Advanced Writers) Students write a timed prompt response without the checklist.	Without referring to the Standing Ovation Checklist, students write a prompt response within a timed twenty-five-minute period. Upon completion, they switch papers with a partner and count how many elements from the checklist are included in the response.

Differentiating Product

Anchor activities

Anchor activities are a solution to the "I'm through, what can I do?" statement that may ring out in your class during the day. In most classrooms, you'll have students who finish their tasks before others, and when they do, it's a good idea to have meaningful assignments available to keep them engaged and on task. Anchor activities are not busy work, but rather extension activities. They focus on the curriculum.

Enactments are done as a group, and response writing is timed, so students aren't likely to have much opportunity to do anchor activities after they finish these tasks. However, enactment-related anchor activities can be a great way to extend the writing curriculum when students finish *other* activities early. For example, students who finish their math early may work on an enactment anchor activity.

One note of caution: there may be times when students rush through their regular assignments in order to work on an anchor activity. In order to keep this from happening, we advise you to place an agreement form next to the anchor activity that students will have to sign, stating that they have finished their work, checked it over, and are satisfied with a job well done. An anchor activity agreement form could look like the one at the bottom left on this page.

Anchor activities to extend and enrich the enactment process might include

1. making theater props for the enactment
2. constructing desktop theaters (see pages 65–67)
3. creating costumes for the enactment
4. searching for new prompts for the class to use
5. writing a longer response or responding to a writing prompt of the student's choice

Choice-as-motivator

This just makes sense: give students choices about the work they do, and they'll take more ownership of their work. They'll work harder, and they'll feel a sense of independence and pride. The enactment process provides natural opportunities for students to make choices. They choose how to enact a given prompt, and they choose how to connect the prompt to their personal lives and how exactly to write about it. Other ways you can give students choices:

- Provide a selection of writing prompts and let them choose which to enact and write about.
- Allow them to find or make up prompts.

Anchor Activity Agreement Form
I am sure that the work I have handed in has been done to the best of my ability and that I have checked it for errors.

Date	Signature	Time of Day

Multiple intelligences

Help your students perform better by working with them to identify their strongest intelligence types and adjusting the enactment process to take advantage of those types.

1. Students with **verbal/linguistic** strengths learn best by listening, talking, and following written directions. These students will thrive when writing prompt responses and working with the Standing Ovation Checklist. You may also allow them to orally plan enactments and write and/or perform dialogue in enactments.

2. Students with **visual/spatial** strengths learn best when working with pictures and models. Allow them to create backdrops, posters, props, and even costumes to be used during enactments.

3. Students with **bodily/kinesthetic** strengths prefer to learn through physical activity. They like to be active. These students will thrive during the enactment, which includes action and dramatization.

4. Students with **logical/mathematical** strengths prefer to learn by applying number, computing, and logic skills. They may be good at choosing precise language and figuring out how to resolve conflicts in enactments and stories.

5. Students with **musical/rhythmic** strengths learn well when they can listen to and engage in music and rhythmic activities. Offer these students the opportunity to infuse vocal and/or instrumental music into the enactment. They may also respond well to musical or poetic writing prompts.

6. Students with **naturalist** strengths prefer to learn by observing and categorizing and exploring the natural world. These students may excel when given the opportunity to act or write about nature.

7. Students with **interpersonal** strengths have "people smarts." They benefit from interacting with other students. Offer these students the chance to work in groups to plan and perform in enactments. They may also benefit from group editing activities after the written responses are finished.

8. Students with **intrapersonal** strengths, who prefer to work alone and think reflectively, may thrive at making personal connections between prompts and their own lives. Allowing these students the opportunity to present soliloquies, rather than group enactments, may be appealing and helpful to them.

Chapter 6
Turning Your Classroom Into a Theater

You can do prompt enactments in your class as simply or extravagantly as you and your students wish. Something simple can be just as effective in triggering personal connections as the most elaborate production. But if you are up for it, making a bigger deal of the process can increase enthusiasm and fun for students. Just using the auditorium stage, if it is available, can lend an air of authenticity and excitement. Venturing outside on a sunny day adds a touch of reality and grabs the attention of the five senses.

● ●

The Classroom Theater

You can also make your own classroom a special place for enactments. Quickly and easily, you can turn your classroom into the perfect theater for your prompt enactments. Simply moving some desks or hanging a curtain over the door will transform your classroom into a stage.

Easily change your classroom into a theater, starting with the seating and stage areas. The process of setting up can be just as important as the finished creation, because setting the stage involves planning, teamwork, and a creative learning environment in which your students may thrive.

Seating and stage areas

Here are two basic seating-and-stage arrangements to consider.

Standard theater setup

> **Stage Area (keep clear)**
>
> If you have a rug in your classroom, you may wish to move it to the front of your room to define the stage floor

> **Traditional Row Seating**
>
> Students may sit at desks in rows or push desks to the back of the classroom and sit in chairs or on the floor.

Theater-in-the-round setup

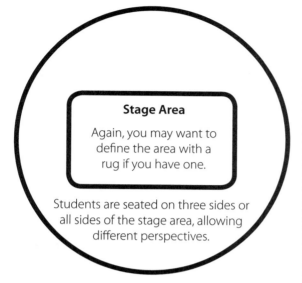

Stage Area

Again, you may want to define the area with a rug if you have one.

Students are seated on three sides or all sides of the stage area, allowing different perspectives.

Stage entrance

A curtain hung over your classroom doorway turns it into a stage entrance and exit. You can use a cloth or paper tablecloth, a bed sheet, a piece of fabric, room divider beads, or anything that will allow you to leave your door open for your students to walk through. Use a spring-loaded curtain rod to hang your curtain. Other possibilities include velcro, bookbinding tape, or other adhesive. Check in with your building maintenance staff before you add anything permanent.

You can also use a curtain over your classroom doorway to serve as a *theater*

entrance. You might have a student "stage crew" setting up the classroom theater while the audience patiently waits outside the door for admittance. You can even give your audience members tickets to the enactments and assign a student as an usher to guide everyone to their seats.

Stage scenery

Once you have displayed your prompt for the class to see, ask students to help create the scenery for the prompt. Visual learners and artistically talented students will jump at the chance to draw on your chalkboard or whiteboard. They may also cut out leaves from construction paper to make one of your students become a tree, or design hats and simple costumes from old pieces of fabric. Students can also paint or draw on poster board, create models with papier-mâché or clay, or do other art projects to create scenery for enactments.

Sound

Invite students to bring in music from home to use as background music or as prompts themselves. (You will want to check out the lyrics before playing a song in class.) You can play CDs on a computer with speakers or a small CD player, or you can play MP3s on a computer or MP3 player. Remember not to play the music too loud during an enactment. You don't want actors to have to shout.

A karaoke machine works well when students have rewritten lyrics or would like to add personal vocals to their presentation. Students may also wish to bring in a CD or MP3 file of sound effects to have on hand for the classroom theater.

Lights

Let the switch on your classroom wall be the source of lighting effects for your stage. You may ask one of your students to blink the lights to signal the beginning of the enactment. Lights may also be turned off to create a night scene. How about a lightning storm? Blink lights on and off quickly. (This may not be appropriate if you have a student who is on the Autism spectrum.) You can use window shades to adjust the light in your room, too. Ask a few of your students to "work the shades."

If your school has an opaque projector, it may be used to shine spotlights or create a colored background. You may purchase clip-on lights at hardware stores or inexpensive holiday lights during the post-holiday sales. Simply darken the room and use your lights for a ghostly glow. Flashlights may be used for this as well.

Props and Costumes

Aside from the stage and setting, you can add life to enactments by providing students with props to interact with or costumes to wear. Even a small accessory or two can make the experience more engaging.

Classroom prop boxes

Start with a classroom prop box—maybe a plastic bin. Keep it filled with items that might be useful as props. Don't be too picky; you'd be surprised what a spatula can become. You can even send notes home to parents asking for donations.

Here are some ideas to get you started:

- Unwanted dance costumes
- Halloween costumes and masks
- Student-made masks
- Old trophies and medals
- Used cell phones
- Kitchen utensils
- Crowns or tiaras
- Toy microphones
- Scarves, hats, and mittens
- Pillowcases
- Bandanas
- Capes
- Plain white painters caps to decorate
- Plain visors to decorate
- Handheld fans to decorate

The possibilities for props are unlimited. In fact, even your prop box itself—or other boxes—can become a prop. If you or someone you know gets a new refrigerator, hurry over to meet the truck. A box that large can be anything from a bus to a castle. That's a valuable box!

Accessories and tools

Tools help your student actors modify and transform the props in your box. Store them together in a gallon plastic bag or shoebox.

- Yarn or string
- Tape (all kinds: scotch, masking, electrical, etc.)
- Scissors
- Safety pins
- Markers, pens, pencils, crayons
- Construction paper
- Aluminum foil
- Feathers
- Craft sticks

Easy-to-make costumes

You and your students can make quick and simple costumes using the following supplies:

- Pillow cases: cut holes for arms and head
- Brown paper shopping bags: cut into vest shapes students can decorate or color

- Large pieces of felt: cut into vests or capes
- Clothing from an older sibling or family adult (with permission, of course)
- Simple face paint kits and narrow paint brushes

Remember to keep the safety of students in mind when selecting these items. Use age-appropriate and developmentally appropriate materials only.

The Desktop Theater

Desktop theaters, made from shoeboxes, can be a fun extension of the physical enactment process. They permit students to create a small stage in which they are not the live star but through which they can still express themselves. Desktop theaters are great for students who may be uncomfortable being on stage but who nonetheless have relevant and important ideas and talent to share with each other and the teacher. Additionally, a desktop theater can be used as a step to support students who may be having difficulty with visualization or weaning themselves off of the live enactment process. Student artists have a venue through which they can apply their artistic skills in the creation of a theater and this confidence will emerge in their written responses.

You can put desktop theaters at learning centers or stations, keep them for small group work, or have each student make one for individual work. Desktop theaters add a fun new way for students to share picture prompts and enact prompts using stick puppets and props. Does it sound simple? It is, and it can bring your students' writing center stage.

For each theater, you'll need:

- One shoebox
- Two pieces of construction paper or fabric, cut to size for curtains
- A dowel, two straws, or a length of string to hold the curtain

You'll also need a hole punch, a box cutter or utility knife, and possibly a pair of scissors or a Phillips-head screwdriver.

Director's Note

Many shoe store employees throw away empty shoeboxes each night. They are often willing to donate the boxes when asked to save them for students. Make a few phone calls or go to your favorite shoe or sneaker emporium and approach the store management about saving the boxes for you. Another source is to ask members of the PTA/ PTO for boxes. You might find that one of these people is in the footwear business with access to boxes.

How to make desktop theaters

Students can easily build these theaters, or you can build them yourself if you don't need too many.

1. Remove the lid from the shoebox and set it aside. Hold the shoebox horizontally (lengthwise) with the opening facing you.

2. Punch one hole on each side panel of the shoebox near the top front of the opening to hold the curtain rod. Depending on the box, a hole punch may not be strong enough to puncture the cardboard. In that case, use the tip of the screwdriver or scissors to bore a hole. Be aware of safety precautions when choosing your tool. An adult may need to puncture the box.

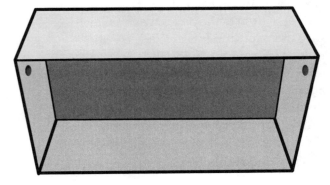

3. Cut the paper or fabric into two pieces. The pieces should be almost as high as the box and about two-thirds as wide. These will be the two stage curtains, one for each side.

4. If your curtain is made from construction paper, fold it as you would a fan, in a back-and-forth fashion. Then cut holes at the top wide enough for your curtain rod to go through. For a fabric curtain, cut holes spaced about two inches apart.

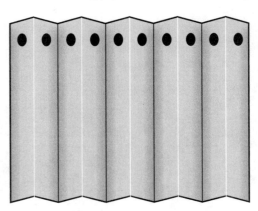

5. Run your curtain rod through the holes of each curtain, so both are hanging from the rod. If you are using straws for your curtain rod, you will need to connect them by slipping one end into another to make them long enough.

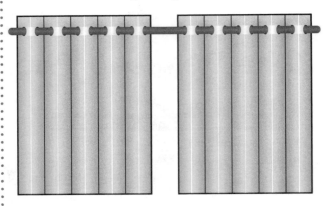

6. Secure the curtain rod to the box by putting one end in one hole and pushing it through far enough so that you can put the other end in the other hole. If you are using string for your curtain rod, string it through the holes and tie the ends together on top of the box.

7. Using the box cutter or utility knife, cut a lengthwise slit along the top of the box toward the back. It should be wide enough to slip picture prompts or background art in and out. Do not allow your students to do this. Work carefully when using this type of knife!

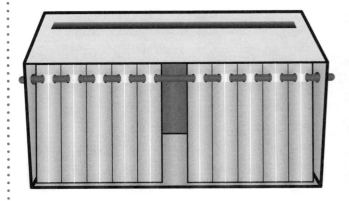

8. Cut a lengthwise slit in the bottom of the box for slipping stick puppets and props in from the bottom.

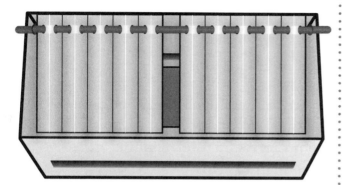

Ways to use the desktop theater

Slide a picture prompt into the slot in back and use it as a fun way to display prompts for individual or small group work. It may be a picture, a textual prompt, or an item related to something mentioned in the prompt. With that in mind, here are some ways to have fun using the desktop theater as an extension of the prompt enactment process.

- Give the box to your students with the curtain closed. When the students open the curtain, they will find their surprise prompt.
- Supply students with a prompt backdrop, stick props, and puppets with which to create their own enactments.
- Ask students to slip a secret backdrop prompt into another student's theater.
- Introduce a new story or concept by using the backdrop as a visual aid. For example, if you are talking about the rain forest, insert a rain forest illustration into the desktop theater. If you are reading a story that takes place in a shoe store, such as Ray Bradbury's short story "The Sound of Summer Running," insert a backdrop that shows shoes. In this way,

the desktop theater can spark discussion prior to reading or writing.

- Display prompts and students' corresponding written responses in theaters throughout the classroom or school, creating a performing arts center. Invite parents and classes to view the theaters. Place a box or catch-all next to the theaters for people to leave words of praise.
- Create a scenery sequence by drawing or mounting pictures on a roll of paper wrapped around toilet paper tubes so it can be advanced through the theater to change prompts or scenery quickly.

Props to use in desktop theaters

Consider adding the following props to desktop theaters for another interesting way to do enactments.

- Dollhouse furniture and characters
- Paper dolls
- Corks that are painted to become goal posts, penguins, snowmen, traffic lights, and other such items
- Stones or leaves
- Motivational erasers in the shape of animals, aliens, etc.
- Toy cars
- Plastic toy farm animals and figures such as cowboys, etc.
- Tiny trophies or medals
- Miniature items mentioned in a written prompt, such as cell phones and sunglasses
- A picture of a prop glued onto a small box (like a jewelry box) or stick. This is useful when you are unable to get the actual prop or the actual item is too big for inside the theater

Chapter 7
Social-Emotional Learning and the Enactment Process

According to CASEL (the Collaborative for Academic, Social, and Emotional Learning), a leading scientific researcher on the subject, social-emotional learning (SEL) can help kids manage their emotions and relationships, understand the emotions of others, make responsible decisions, handle challenges, feel less emotional distress, make friends, and reduce conflicts. It can also help improve kids' academic performance—including achievement test scores. These are important lifelong skills.

The enactment process can be a powerful SEL tool, helping students gain skills that build confidence and self-esteem, work out conflicts, and improve learning.

How the Enactment Process Supports SEL

The enactment process promotes social-emotional awareness and development in many ways. A prime way is by helping students explore and understand their own feelings and those of others.

When first presented with the idea of a prompt enactment, students might feel anxious about standing in front of their peers to act. It is important to acknowledge these feelings as normal and quite common. You might even wish to create a chart or list of the many feelings that the idea of enacting might lead to and a corresponding list of possible reasons why the students might be feeling these ways. This is a wonderful way for students to see they are not alone in these feelings.

A main benefit of this discussion is simply the emotionally safe environment you are providing within your classroom. Since you are working as a class and talking in general terms, students can feel safe talking about feelings and explore the reasons for them. They are not being put on the spot or talking specifically about their own feelings. Be sure you acknowledge that you and the class will be supportive and nonjudgmental about all feelings students have.

Another benefit is the help you give students in articulating their feelings. You can provide the vocabulary students need to talk about how they feel. (Feelings words make terrific spelling words! Make sure that the words are representative of both positive and negative emotions.)

Finally, this discussion is a perfect opportunity for you to provide students with skills and hints to overcoming performance anxiety or fears about personal expression. Some suggestions might include:

- doing the first enactment with a friend (or with you)
- doing the first enactment in mime, without dialogue
- closing your eyes and breathing deeply before the enactment
- making believe everyone in the class has a silly mask on when you look at them

Students can use these skills to overcome test-taking anxiety, too. In fact, simply doing enactments in front of the class is great preparation. Once students learn to harness their emotions during enactments, they can apply those same strategies to staying calm during tests. They also are likely to develop a sense of confidence about writing, allowing them to work with confidence during the test.

Not all students will feel anxious about their first enactment. Most classrooms have at least one child who will be jumping out of his or her seat to be the first one to act out a scene. You might want to ask enthusiastic students to talk about how they feel and why they feel that way.

Encouraging empathy

It is very important that all students know they will be supported by their classmates when it is their turn to enact. Prior to the first enactment, you may wish to discuss how professional actors might feel if members of the audience started talking to the person next to them during the performance, or if they started to behave rudely. Once again, consider creating a list of words describing how the actor might feel. These words might include the following: *frustrated, angry, perplexed, insulted, confused,* and *humiliated.*

This discussion helps students develop empathy. It also helps them understand their roles as audience members. The students in your class must know that being an audience member involves respectful, active listening and watching.

Although feelings of nervousness about speaking or performing in front of a group may never completely go away, these feelings are usually replaced by a sense of pride and accomplishment for most students when they finish their enactment—especially if you are sure to give the actors a round of applause. "Fan mail" can also be encouraging for the actors and help audience members analyze performances for strengths. See page 22.

Other ways the enactment process supports SEL

Throughout the year, the enactment process will help students:

- understand the feelings of others as they bring a prompt to life
- understand that everyone reacts differently to situations as evidenced in different enactments to the same prompt
- learn to work in groups in order to enact the prompt
- understand and accept responsibility for their obligation to and role within their enactment group
- understand that one's actions have consequences, sometimes on others' feelings
- develop empathy by putting themselves "in someone else's shoes"
- learn to express themselves effectively both orally and in writing
- recognize strengths in themselves and their classmates
- manage emotions to handle pressure situations appropriately
- understand the difference between thinking, feeling, and acting
- improve their self-image through positive activity
- persuade another person to see things from a different perspective

Aligning the Enactment Process with Illinois Goals, Standards, and Descriptors for SEL

Goal 1: Develop self-awareness and self-management skills to achieve school and life success.

Standard and Descriptor	Addressed During the Enactment Process
Standard 1A: Identify and manage one's emotions and behavior. **Descriptor 5:** Demonstrate emotions in various contexts in role plays.	Students demonstrate emotions when they become a character in a prompt.
Standard 1A, Descriptor 6: Practice handling pressure situations (e.g., taking a test, participating in a competitive activity).	Students perform enactments, a pressure situation. To prepare for the assessment, students take timed writing tests; teachers cover up posters and other support items before the test to simulate the real testing situation.
Standard 1B: Recognize personal qualities and external supports. **Descriptor 4:** Recognize that students learn differently.	Working in groups, students learn to collaborate according to one another's strengths and weaknesses. Students edit each other's writing.
Standard 1C: Demonstrate skills related to achieving personal and academic goals. **Descriptor 4:** Monitor progress on planned action steps for an academic goal.	Students monitor the progress of their mastery of the Standing Ovation Checklist skills.

Goal 2: Use social awareness and interpersonal skills to establish and maintain positive relationships.

Standard and Descriptor	Addressed During the Enactment Process
Standard 2A: Recognize the feelings and perspectives of others. **Descriptor 4:** Ask open-ended questions to encourage others to express themselves.	Students ask open-ended questions of enactors and each other when they participate as part of the audience.
Standard 2A, Descriptor 5: Role-play the perspectives of various characters in scenarios provided.	Students take on the perspectives of many characters during enactments.
Standard 2C: Use communication and social skills to interact effectively with others. **Descriptor 5:** Demonstrate support for others' contributions to a group/team effort.	As members of the audience, students learn to supporte each others' efforts, including by giving enactors a round of applause after every enactment.

Goal 3: Demonstrate decision-making skills and responsible behaviors in personal, school, and community contexts.

Standard and Descriptor	Addressed During the Enactment Process
Standard 3B: Apply decision-making skills to deal responsibly with daily academic and social situations. **Descriptor 5:** Demonstrate an ability to stay on task.	Students demonstrate this ability during visualization and self-editing, as well as when they write responses that remain within the topic of the prompt.

Illinois SEL goals, standards, and descriptors used with permission of the Illinois State Board of Education (ISBE). The ISBE does not endorse this book.

- practice strategies for conflict resolution
- set long-term and short-term goals

Illinois is a leading state in developing SEL standards. The table on page 70 shows a selection of the Illinois SEL goals, standards, and descriptors for late elementary and junior high school, and how different aspects of the prompt enactment process address them. Complete standards are available at www .isbe.net/ils/social_emotional/standards.htm.

Using SEL-Specific Writing Prompts

In addition to the many ways the enactment process supports SEL in and of itself, you can take the benefits even further by assigning prompts with SEL themes. These prompts might be adapted from a story or book you read in class or from a situation that happens in class. You might simply invent prompts with moral or ethical dilemmas built in, or with opportunities for self-reflection or problem-solving.

Photographs are another fertile source of SEL-based writing prompts. Bring in pictures that show a person or people displaying a strong emotion such as sadness, fear, or anger. You can find many such pictures online or in newspapers, magazines, or even your own photo albums. Place the photos in a desktop theater if you like. (See pages 65–67.) Ask students to enact the picture, perhaps speculating what happened before or after. This would make a great speculative prompt response.

If your students are working on persuasive writing, discussing and writing about issues important to them can help them learn a lot about managing emotions and empathizing with others. Assignments like these can also give them experience exploring their own feelings and opinions. A great source for issues and arguments is letters to the editor. It's easy to find many letters to the editor at newspaper Web sites. Ask students to read and reply to a letter with an argument for or against the writer's point of view. Or have them come up with their own issues and write letters.

It's important to help students make arguments in a respectful way, especially if they are taking opinions contrary to those of classmates. Model respectful listening and discussing.

Following are several other activities you can do to promote SEL through the enactment process.

Hey, what's happening?

Have your actors enact a scene that deals with a social-emotional issue, such as bullying, teasing, or sportsmanship, and stop the enactment before any conclusion is reached. Then ask your students to write about how they would handle the situation. Alternatively, you could have the actors decide how they would handle the situation and conclude the enactment by showing that ending (including their emotional reaction). Students writing could then write about any of the following:

- whether they agree with how the actors handled the situation
- how they would handle the situation
- a similar personal situation

The "What's Happening" cards on page 74 contain prompts you can use for this enactment. Or you can make up your own prompts—perhaps regarding a situation currently affecting your classroom. Students, too, can be encouraged to write prompts, thus bringing many issues to light that you may not have known about.

Copy or print out the cards, laminate them to make them last longer, and cut them out. You can have students choose a card randomly or you can assign them.

You can also reverse the enactment process for a twist on an SEL activity. Have students write about a situation in which they felt a strong emotion, then have volunteers enact the scenario. This allows students to see their words brought to life, which can validate their feelings and raise self-confidence.

Emotion commotion

Emotion commotion requires students to write about the impact of emotions and attitudes on various tasks. Once enacted, your students will be able to see firsthand how attitude and emotion play important roles in the outcome of even the most basic of situations.

Write various individual emotions on index cards and place them in a bag or bowl. If you like, you can use the "How You Feel About It" cards provided on page 75. Next, write various situations on separate index cards and place them in a second bag or bowl. You can use the "What You Are Doing" cards on page 76.

Ask your students to choose one card from each bag and enact a scene combining the two cards. For example, the combination of the two cards "Eager" and "Walking home from school" would set the stage for students to enact a scene telling why they were eager to walk home, and how their eagerness affected their walk. If the cards "Afraid" and "Walking home from school" are chosen, this would set the stage for a totally different enactment—even though students would be doing the same activity (walking home).

You can modify this activity in many ways to meet the needs and interests of your students. You could spend an entire class period enacting one card from the "What You Are Doing" bag, each with a different "How You Feel About It" card. Each group would enact the same situation from a different emotional perspective, helping students understand how powerfully emotions can impact the same situation.

Similarly, you can have students select a single "How You Feel About It" card and enact various situations for that feeling. This shows how a feeling can affect nearly everything you do. If you are sad, for instance, this sadness can influence your whole day.

I found it! Is it mine?

Give students an envelope filled with fake money and ask them to enact a scenario in which this is real money that they just found. To practice speculative writing, have students write about who the money belonged to before they found it and how this person would feel after realizing the money is lost. To practice persuasive writing, have students write a letter to their teacher in an attempt to convince this adult either to allow them to keep the found money or to help them find the owner.

Apology methodology

From the time they were very young, many kids have been told to apologize when they do something wrong or if they hurt someone's feelings. The imposed apology usually comes in the form of the two-word response "I'm sorry." Many students feel those two simple words "take them off the hook," and once they've said them, everything is automatically fixed: their wrong has been righted. Other students view the words "I'm sorry" as a sign of weakness, or a statement of inferiority.

Apology methodology lets students explore and understand the meaning and purpose of an apology. It begins with a discussion of what an apology is, how it feels to give one, and how it feels to receive one. A genuine apology includes an acknowledgment of what the speaker did and how it felt to the other person. It also includes a promise to try to do better in the future. When we teach children how to apologize, they learn not only how to do it effectively, but also how good it feels to receive such a genuine apology. Once they understand the power of it, they may be more inclined to use the strategy themselves.

After discussing how to apologize, pass out an index card to each student (or small group). Ask students to write on the cards a brief description of a situation that would warrant an apology, without actually writing the apology. Put the situation cards in a bag or place facedown on a desk.

Next, ask students or groups to select a card and enact the situation described. At the end of the enactment, have a class discussion about how the person who needs to apologize could do so, and what else the person might do to make things better. Students may then write about how they would have handled the situation if they had been involved.

This type of enactment can teach strategies for both giving and accepting apologies. An interesting speculative prompt may be to ask students to write about what would happen to the relationship of the characters in the enactment if no apology is made. An interesting persuasive prompt may be for the students to write a letter telling one of the characters in the prompt why they should accept the apology.

Using song lyrics as prompts

Song lyrics can be wonderful prompts for enacting and writing about social-emotional issues. Identify age-appropriate songs about emotions or emotional situations, play them in class, and provide lyrics for students either as a handout or projected on the wall.

A song can be a prompt on its own, much like a poetry prompt, but you can also create entire sets of prompts around a particular song. For example, the song "Hero" by Mariah Carey makes for a great song/poetry prompt. This song is about looking inside oneself to find courage in the face of

fear, sorrow, and adversity; it's about being strong and believing in yourself. You can have students write stories about times they acted heroic or about a person in their lives they consider a hero. You can follow this up with a speculative prompt asking students to write about what a hero would do in a certain situation or what it would be like to meet their hero. Next, you can provide a picture of a hero as a picture prompt (or ask students to bring in pictures of heroes—real or imaginary—that they want to write about).

Many songs deal with themes of tolerance, responsibility, keeping secrets, empathy and sympathy, and putting yourself in someone else's shoes. Remember to preview the lyrics before you share them with class. Here is a short list of appropriate songs, along with a summary of their SEL themes, to get you started:

- "Hero," Mariah Carey (courage, self-confidence)
- "Man in the Mirror," Michael Jackson (self-improvement, personal responsibility)
- "Unwritten," Natasha Bedingfield (empathy, self-expression, individuality)
- "Lean on Me," Bill Withers (helping others, being a good friend)
- "Thank You for Being a Friend," Andrew Gold (gratitude, appreciation for friendship)
- "Ebony and Ivory," Paul McCartney and Stevie Wonder (tolerance)
- "Greatest Love of All," Whitney Houston (pride, belief in self, personal strength)
- "Father and Daughter," Paul Simon (parental love, importance of family)
- "Because You Loved Me," Céline Dion (appreciation of parent)
- "Here Comes the Sun," the Beatles (excitement, anticipation, appreciation of nature)
- "No," They Might Be Giants (frustration of being a kid)

What's Happening

You see your best friend cheating on a test.

What's Happening

You hurt your friend's feelings, and you apologized right away, but your friend is still mad at you.

What's Happening

Your sister is supposed to stay home with you while your parents are out. Instead, she goes out with her boyfriend and you are left alone.

What's Happening

You are on a social networking Web site and see that someone is spreading mean rumors about you.

What's Happening

Your friends are going to the fair on Friday night, and you are asking your parents if you may go, too (without a chaperone).

What's Happening

You asked your friend to return your favorite CD that he or she borrowed, but your friend tells you it's lost.

What's Happening

You see a student take something out of another student's locker.

What's Happening

You are friends with two people who don't like each other, and you want them both to come to your party.

What's Happening

You want to belong to the Book Club at school, but your friends say you will be a nerd if you join.

What's Happening

You are at a store with friends, and one of them takes something without paying for it.

What's Happening

You worked very hard on a report and got a "C" on it. Your friend copied the entire report and got an A+.

What's Happening

You really want to quit the team, but you are the best player and they will lose without you.

What's Happening

Your school will not allow students to wear denim to class. Most of your pants are jeans.

What's Happening

Your best friend has stopped talking to you and won't tell you why.

What's Happening

The toughest kid in school cuts in front of you every day in the cafeteria.

What's Happening

You are blamed for something you didn't do.

What's Happening

How You Feel About It

Happy	Sad	Relieved	Afraid
How You Feel About It	How You Feel About It	How You Feel About It	How You Feel About It
Proud	Embarrassed	Excited	Frustrated
How You Feel About It	How You Feel About It	How You Feel About It	How You Feel About It
Angry	Regretful	Envious	Worried
How You Feel About It	How You Feel About It	How You Feel About It	How You Feel About It
Confident	Grateful	Eager	Enthusiastic
How You Feel About It	How You Feel About It	How You Feel About It	How You Feel About It

What You Are Doing

Homework	Household chores	Texting a friend	Watching TV
What You Are Doing	What You Are Doing	What You Are Doing	What You Are Doing
Eating lunch	Walking home from school	Playing video games	Shopping for clothes
What You Are Doing	What You Are Doing	What You Are Doing	What You Are Doing
Mowing the lawn	Cooking	Reading a book	Taking a test
What You Are Doing	What You Are Doing	What You Are Doing	What You Are Doing
Riding your bicycle	Baby-sitting your little sister	Listening to music	Dancing
What You Are Doing	What You Are Doing	What You Are Doing	What You Are Doing

Part 3

The Types of Writing Prompts

Chapter 8
The Picture Prompt

The picture prompt provides a visual image for students to write about. They are expected to write a narrative account of what is happening in the picture—a story with a beginning, middle, and end. Their stories should include all the elements on the Standing Ovation Checklist for Picture Prompts (page 82).

Even if your state's assessment does not include a picture prompt, we recommend that you use the picture prompt to teach your students the enactment process. It is the easiest way to introduce the process, because students look at the image and simply enact what they see. The progression of the image from the page to the enactment to the image students create in their minds is clear and obvious. Once students understand that a writing prompt should create an image in their minds, it will be easier for them to write responses. Then they are ready to tackle text prompts, which require them to imagine the image before they enact it.

Picture Sources

For most of the year, you can use the picture prompts provided in Part 4 of this book, on pages 118–127, or you can find your own. Make finding prompts part of your classroom activity. The more students are engaged in the pictures themselves, the more readily they'll engage in the writing process.

You can find pictures almost anywhere, and most of the time they're free. Save old greeting cards and calendars; their photos and illustrations can be interesting and colorful. Look through newspapers and magazines for photos from current events stories, destination shots from the travel section, or the latest toys from advertisements. Comic books contain wonderful characters for students to write about. You may even use CD covers.

Using illustrations from books or stories your students haven't read yet is an excellent way to build excitement about an upcoming story. Don't use a picture or illustration from a story that students already know, because they usually will just retell the story the author wrote. Use a picture from an unknown story, and students will create something different from what they will read. They might even like their story better than the author's!

Students can be a great help for finding pictures. Ask them to keep their eyes open for pictures they think would be interesting to write about. Send a note home asking for family contributions as well, including family photos from vacations or important events. Or ask students to draw original pictures.

If your students' assessment test uses picture prompts, you will eventually want to start using picture prompts that more accurately reflect the prompts they'll find on the test. You may be able to find the picture prompts used in previous tests. See pages 44–45.

Enacting the Prompt

When preparing for the enactment process with a picture prompt, be sure your students understand what kind of writing will be expected: a fictional narrative about the picture they will see. The enactment process is discussed in greater detail in chapter 2.

See It

Step 1: View the prompt

Show your students the prompt, preferably by hanging a large poster or projecting a large image. Be sure everyone can see the picture clearly. Give your students about two minutes to study the picture. Here's an example:

Step 2: Discuss the prompt

After two minutes, have a class discussion about what students see in the picture. This is a brainstorming session, so explain that there are no right or wrong answers and all ideas are valued. It should be a lively, non-judgmental discussion. The point is to get students thinking critically and creatively about the prompt.

Be It

Step 3: Enact the prompt

Ask for volunteers from the class to enact the prompt. Depending on the level of confidence and skill in your class, you may have them simply create a frozen image of the picture, mime a simple action, or act out a full scene including dialogue. Have them become the characters in the picture, and maybe even the props, if appropriate. For example, students enacting the baseball prompt could play the roles of the umpire, catcher, and batter.

Remind the other students to actively observe the enactment and to think about what is happening in the picture. They participate as active members of the audience.

Step 4: Discuss the enactment

While students are enacting the scene, use the checklist to guide a discussion about the early elements in the story, including the hook and story beginning. Whether you will scribe a story as a group or students will write on their own, you will want to take notes on the ideas you come up with either on the board, on chart paper, or somewhere else.

Ask students, "If this picture could talk, who would be talking and what would we hear?" Depending on how your discussion goes, actors may change positions, speak as if in character, and evolve the scene. This shows your students how a story can evolve and how several stories can come from one picture.

Here is a list of general discussion questions to use with most picture prompts:

- What are the characters doing?
- What are the names of the characters?
- What are their ages?
- How do the characters know each other? Are they members of a family or friends?
- Why are they there?
- What problem or situation are the characters facing or involved in?
- What is the setting (time and location) of the scene?

You may want to ask more specific questions about the individual picture you are using. A good way to start is by asking if any of the students have any experience doing or seeing the topic in the picture. Then get deeper into characters' heads than you did with the general questions, using the context of the picture to help form questions about what characters might be thinking or doing. Finally, mention parts of the physical scene. What details can students come up with for the five senses?

For the baseball prompt and enactment, ask students questions like the following to get students thinking critically about the picture and relating it to their own personal experiences. It may only take one or two questions to get your class talking about the picture and making their own picture-to-self, picture-to-text, or picture-to-world connections.

- Have any of you been to a baseball game?
- Have you been a player or a fan?
- What are the jobs of the people in this picture?
- Where are they?
- Why are they there?
- Do the players know each other? How?
- What is the umpire saying? (You may also be addressing new vocabulary such as the word *umpire*.)
- What is the catcher thinking?
- What is the batter thinking?
- Will he hit the ball or strike out?
- Who are the fans?
- Why are the fans there?
- What are they saying?
- What are the names of the teams?
- What are the names of the players and the umpire?
- What happened before the batter stepped up to the plate?
- What will happen after he hits the ball?
- What will happen after the game?
- Is this an important game?

- How does the batter feel at this very moment?
- How does the catcher feel at this very moment?
- How does the umpire feel at this very moment?
- What do you see, hear, touch, taste, and smell at a baseball game?
- What does it feel like to sit in the stands?
- What do you eat at a baseball game?

Step 5: A round of applause

Let your actors sit down, and have the class give them a round of applause.

Step 6: Write or scribe a prompt response

Ask your students to look again at the original prompt. If you turned off the projector or removed the image, make it available again for everyone to view. This is important because during the assessment test the students will be looking at a picture, not a live enactment.

If you will be scribing a story with your students, have them gather around the chart pad and easel. Use the ideas from your discussion to draft the hook and beginning section of your story. Refer to pages 23–26 for how to proceed from the beginning to the middle to the end of the scribed story.

If students are writing on their own, have them begin working while ideas are fresh in their minds. The enactment often sparks enthusiasm, because students get excited about the many options they have for telling a story about the characters. Emphasize to students that they aren't just writing a description of a picture but rather a story about an event or experience. It is a personal story about a moment in time.

Step 7: Self-edit the response

Once the written responses are finished, it is time for students to edit them. If you have scribed a response, you can self-edit as a group. If students have written on their own, the self-editing can be done a number of ways, all of which begin with the Standing Ovation Checklist for Picture Prompts.

- You may ask students to code their stories to the checklist (see page 82 and the CD-ROM for a reproducible handout of the checklist; see page 37 for more on coding written responses).
- You may have students trade with a partner and code each other's responses. It is often easier for students to edit someone else's work than their own.
- You may have students work in pairs or groups using the appropriate Standing Ovation Checklist Playing Cards (see pages 47–52).

Once a student's response is coded, he or she should revise the piece, adding any missing elements. Students may also embellish ideas or add entirely new ideas. If you are practicing for the test, encourage them not to add too much or write entirely new drafts, because they may run out of time. But for other assignments during the year, you may want to require clean new second drafts.

If students are struggling with how to add a particular element, make sure they know they can seek help from you or another classroom assistant. While students are self-editing, walk among them, checking in about their progress and comfort with the writing prompt and checklist. You may call a few students together for a mini-lesson on a common need.

The Standing Ovation Checklist

For Picture Prompts

	Yes	No
1. The story has a setting.		
2. Characters in the story have names.		
3. The beginning is a "hook" for the reader.		
4. The characters in the story have a problem or conflict.		
5. Dialogue, punctuated correctly, is included in the story.		
6. At least two of the three forms of ending punctuation are included in the story: period (.), question mark (?), and exclamation point (!).		
7. The story contains broad and accurate vocabulary.		
8. The story includes action and rich details.		
9. The story stays on the topic of the prompt.		
10. The problem or conflict is resolved by the end of the story.		
11. Each new paragraph is indented.		
12. The story has been written neatly.		
13. The title is related to the story.		
14.		
15.		

Chapter 9
The Speculative Prompt

The speculative prompt is similar to the picture prompt in that students are asked to apply creative writing skills to write a narrative story with a beginning, middle, and end. But unlike the picture prompt, the speculative prompt is a piece of text rather than a picture. In response to a speculative prompt, students may be asked to write a story in which they are a participant or character. Other times, students may be asked to write a response in which all the characters are fictional, similar to a response to a picture prompt. Student stories should include all the elements on the Standing Ovation Checklist for Speculative Prompts (page 87; the elements on this list are identical to those on the picture prompt list).

Speculative Prompt Sources

For most of the year, you can use the speculative prompts provided in Part 4 of this book, on pages 128–137, or you can find your own. Make finding prompts part of your classroom activity. The more students are engaged in the prompts themselves, the more readily they'll engage in the writing process.

To find speculative prompt ideas, look for paragraphs or smaller bits of text that lend themselves to speculation. Perhaps a person is faced with a decision, someone is wondering what to do next or how something happened, or someone states an opinion or something they have learned. You can find paragraphs like these in news or feature articles, your language arts anthology, and text books (such as history books). You might find them on age-appropriate Web sites or blogs. Perhaps you can find speculative prompts in song lyrics. (Make sure you read the lyrics before presenting them to your class.)

You can easily find suspenseful situations in fictional sources such as chapter books, comic books, graphic novels, and other sources. If you are reading a story as a class, one way to approach this is to stop the story at a suspenseful point, or a point where a decision needs to be made. Then go through the enactment process using the part of the story you have read thus far as the prompt. Students can enact and write about what they think will happen next. When finished, return to the real story and finish it. Students can even discuss which ending they liked best—the one they thought of or the one that really happened in the story.

Finally, consider inventing your own speculative prompts from scratch. Students love to do this, too. Once everyone gets the hang of it, you can have a lot of fun coming up with dilemmas and other speculative prompts.

If your students will be responding to speculative prompts on their assessment test, you will eventually want to start using prompts that more accurately reflect those they'll find on the test. As with picture prompts, you may be able to find speculative prompts used in previous tests. See pages 44–45.

Enacting the Prompt

When preparing for the enactment process with a speculative prompt, be sure your students understand what kind of writing will be expected: a fictional narrative about the situation they read about. The enactment process is discussed in greater detail in chapter 2.

Step 1: View the prompt

Show your students the prompt, preferably by hanging a large poster or projecting a large image on the wall. Be sure everyone can see the prompt clearly. Read the prompt aloud, then give your students a couple minutes to read it silently to themselves and think about it. Here's an example of a speculative prompt:

See It

You've just won a million dollars! You will receive the money in a lump sum next week. The catch is that you must share it with one person—an even fifty-fifty split. Write about who you choose and what you will do with your share of the money.

Step 2: Discuss the prompt

After two minutes, have a class discussion about who and what students see in their mental images of the scenario. This is a brainstorming session, so explain that there are no right or wrong answers and all ideas are valued. It should be a lively, nonjudgmental discussion. The point is to get students thinking critically and creatively about the prompt.

Step 3: Enact the prompt

Ask for volunteers from the class to enact the prompt. Depending on the level of confidence and skill in your class, you may have them simply create a frozen image that they come up with, mime a simple action, or act out a full scene including dialogue. They should become the characters in the scenario, and maybe even the props, if appropriate. For example, students enacting the prompt about the million dollars could play the roles of the winner and the two friends she had to choose between to share the money with.

Remind the other students to actively observe the enactment and to think about what is happening. They participate as active members of the audience.

Step 4: Discuss the enactment

While students are enacting the scene, use the checklist to guide a discussion about the early elements in the story, including the hook and story beginning. Whether you will scribe a story as a group or students will write on their own, you will want to take notes on the ideas you come up with either on the board, on chart paper, or somewhere else.

Ask students, "If you won a million dollars, how would you feel and what would you say?" Depending on how your discussion goes, actors may change positions, speak as if in character, and evolve the scene. This shows your students how a story can evolve and how several stories can come from one prompt.

Here is a list of general discussion questions to use with most speculative prompts:

- What are the characters doing?
- What are the names of the characters?
- What are their ages?
- How do the characters know each other? Are they members of a family or friends?
- Why are they there?
- What problem or situation are the characters facing or involved in?
- What is the setting (time and location) of the scene?

You may want to ask more specific questions about the individual prompt you are using. A good way to start is by asking if any of the students have any experience with the topic posed in the prompt. Then get deeper into characters' heads than you did with the general questions, using the context of the prompt to help form questions about what characters might be thinking or doing.

Finally, mention parts of the physical scene. What details can students mention for each of the five senses?

For the million dollars prompt and enactment, ask students questions like the following to get students thinking critically about the scenario and relating it to their own personal experiences. It may only take one or two questions to get your class talking about the prompt and making their own text-to-self, text-to-text, or text-to-world connections.

- Have any of you ever won a prize?
- What did you win?
- How did you feel about winning?
- What did you say or do when you won?
- Has anyone ever shared something important with you?
- Have you shared something important with someone else?
- How did you decide who to share with?
- How did you feel about sharing?
- How do you think you won the million dollars?
- Who would you share it with? Why?
- What will you do with your half of the money? Why?

- How will the person whom you selected feel about being chosen?
- What would $1,000,000 feel like or look like?
- Would you save any of it or spend it all? Why?
- Would it change your life? How or why?

Step 5: A round of applause

Let your actors sit down, and have the class give them a round of applause.

Step 6: Write or scribe a prompt response

Ask your students to read the original prompt again. If you turned off the projector or removed the prompt, make it available again for everyone to view. This is important because during the assessment test the students will be looking at a few sentences on a page, not a live enactment.

If you will be scribing a story with your students, have them gather around the chart pad and easel. Use the ideas from your discussion to draft the hook and beginning section of your story. Refer to pages 23–26 for how to proceed from the beginning to the middle to the end of the scribed story.

If students are writing on their own, have them begin working while ideas are fresh in their minds. The enactment often sparks enthusiasm, because students get excited about the many options they have for telling a story about the characters. Emphasize to students that they aren't just writing a description of a scenario or decision but rather a story about an event or experience. It is a story about a moment in time.

Step 7: Self-edit the response

Once the written responses are finished, it is time for students to edit them. If you have scribed a response, you can self-edit as a group. If students have written on their own, the self-editing can be done a number of ways, all of which begin with the Standing Ovation Checklist for Speculative Prompts.

- You may ask students to code their stories to the checklist (see page 91 and the CD-ROM for a reproducible handout of the checklist; see page 37 for more on coding written responses).
- You may have students trade with a partner and code each other's responses. It is often easier for students to edit someone else's work than their own.
- You may have students work in pairs or groups using the appropriate Standing Ovation Checklist Playing Cards (see pages 47–52).

Once a student's response is coded, he or she should revise the piece, adding any missing elements. Students may also embellish ideas or add entirely new ideas. If you are practicing for the test, encourage them not to add too much or to write entirely new drafts, since they may run out of time. But for other assignments during the year, you may want to require clean second drafts.

If students are struggling with how to add a particular element, make sure they know they can seek help from you or another classroom assistant. While students are self-editing, walk among them, checking in about their progress and comfort with the writing prompt and checklist. You may call a few students together for a mini-lesson on a common need.

The Standing Ovation Checklist

For Speculative Prompts

	Yes	No
1. The story has a setting.		
2. Characters in the story have names.		
3. The beginning is a "hook" for the reader.		
4. The characters in the story have a problem or conflict.		
5. Dialogue, punctuated correctly, is included in the story.		
6. At least two of the three forms of ending punctuation are included in the story: period (.), question mark (?), and exclamation point (!).		
7. The story contains broad and accurate vocabulary.		
8. The story includes action and rich details.		
9. The story stays on the topic of the prompt.		
10. The problem or conflict is resolved by the end of the story.		
11. Each new paragraph is indented.		
12. The story has been written neatly.		
13. The title is related to the story.		
14.		
15.		

Chapter 10
The Persuasive Prompt

Persuasive prompts describe an issue and require students to choose a side and make an argument for that side. Typically, student responses are written in the form of a letter addressed to a person mentioned in the prompt. A good argument is supported by at least three reasons and acknowledges another point of view. Responses should include all the elements on the Standing Ovation Checklist for Persuasive Prompts, which contains several elements not included on the checklists for picture and speculative prompts. See pages 94–95.

Persuasive Prompt Sources

For most of the year, you can use the persuasive prompts provided in Part 4 of this book, on pages 138–147, or you can find your own. Make finding prompts part of your classroom activity. The more students are engaged in the prompts themselves, the more readily they'll engage in the writing process.

To find persuasive prompt ideas, check out editorials and letters to the editor on newspaper Web sites. Ask students to read one and reply with an argument for or against the writer's point of view. You can also have students come up with their own issues and write letters. Or, using TV and movie sections of newspapers or Web sites as a model, students may write a review arguing why they liked or didn't like a movie, book, or TV show.

Finally, it can be a lot of fun to invent your own persuasive prompts from scratch. Students love to do this, too. As a class, brainstorm issues that are important to the students and that provoke them to take sides. School policies on issues such as dress code, homework, cell phones, and recess can be fertile ground for such discussions.

If your students will be responding to persuasive prompts on their assessment test, you will eventually want to start using prompts that more accurately reflect those they'll find on the test. You may be able to find persuasive prompts used in previous tests. See pages 44–45.

Enacting the Prompt

When preparing for the enactment process with a persuasive prompt, be sure your students understand what kind of writing will be expected: an argument for one side of the issue they read about. The argument needs to be supported by at least three reasons, so they should be thinking about reasons while observing or participating in the enactment. The enactment process is discussed in greater detail in chapter 2.

Step 1: View the prompt

Show your students the prompt, preferably by hanging a large poster or projecting the text of the prompt. Be sure everyone can see the prompt clearly. Read the prompt aloud, then give your students a couple minutes to read it silently to themselves and think about it. The "See It" bubble on this page shows an example of a persuasive prompt.

Step 2: Discuss the prompt

After two minutes, have a class discussion about who and what students see in their mental images of the scenario. This is a brainstorming session, so explain that there are no right or wrong answers and all ideas are valued. It should be a lively, nonjudgmental discussion. The point is to get students thinking critically and creatively about the prompt. They should think about the stance they will take on the issue and what reasons they might use to support that stance. They should also think about alternate points of view. They should prepare to argue using facts and substantiating details that persuade the reader to understand and accept their point of view.

See It

The principal of your school is upset with the way the building looks at the end of the school day. Students' papers and trash are scattered in the hallways, and things look generally messy. The principal's solution is for every student to spend half an hour a week working with a member of the custodial staff.

How do you feel about this situation and the principal's solution? Take a stance and write a letter to the principal expressing whether you agree or disagree with the plan. Use details and examples to support your point of view.

Step 3: Enact the prompt

Ask for volunteers from the class to enact the prompt. Depending on the level of confidence and skill in your class, you may have them simply create a frozen image that they come up with, mime a simple action, or act out a full scene including dialogue. They should become the characters in the scenario, and maybe even the props, if appropriate. For example, students enacting the messy school prompt might choose to enact a scene where students carelessly leave their trash in the hallways or they might choose to enact what it would be like for a student to work with a custodian.

Remind the other students to actively observe the enactment and to think about what is happening in the picture. They participate as active members of the audience.

Step 4: Discuss the enactment

While students are enacting the scene, use the checklist to guide a discussion about the early elements in the story, including the hook; the stances writers can take; and reasons to support the stances. Whether you will scribe a story as a group or students will write on their own, you will want to take notes on the ideas generated on the board, on chart paper, or somewhere else.

Ask students, "If our principal made this rule, how would you feel?" Depending on how your discussion goes, actors may change positions, speak as if in character, and evolve the scene. This shows your students how a persuasive response can evolve and how there can be more than one response to one prompt.

Here is a list of general discussion questions to use with most persuasive prompts:

- Who are the characters in the scenario (this refers to any people in the enactment as well as the person to whom the letter is going to be addressed)?
- What are the names of the characters?
- What are their ages?

- How do the characters know each other?
- What is the time and location of the prompt?
- What are the characters doing?
- Why are they there?
- What problem or situation are the characters facing or involved in?
- Have you ever written a letter to voice your opinion about a topic? Who did you write to, and why? What was the result?
- What is the purpose of your letter? What do you want to accomplish by writing this letter?
- Who are you sending the letter to? Who is the audience for your letter?
- What is the format of a friendly letter?

You may want to ask more specific questions about the individual prompt you are using, in particular about which side of the issue students want to take. A good way to start is by asking if any of the students have any experience with the issue raised in the prompt or issues similar to it. Go further by asking students what feelings the issue has evoked in them or might evoke. Talk about reasons why the issue has come up and possible ways to resolve it. How might people other than the students themselves be affected by the issue and the suggested solutions?

For the messy school prompt, ask students the following questions to get them thinking critically about the issue and relating it to their own personal experiences. Your discussion may help students formulate their opinions and analyze their reasons for supporting their opinions. It may only take one or two questions to get your class talking about the prompt and making their own text-to-self, text-to-text, or text-to-world connections.

- Has your mom, dad, or other adult ever been upset with a messy room at home?

- What responsibilities do you have for cleaning up at home? What happens if you don't take care of your responsibilities?

- Do you think your school is dirty or clean at the end of the school day? Why?

- Do you think that keeping the school clean is your responsibility? Defend your position.

- Is it fair for the principal to make all students help clean up? Why or why not?

- Should students be teamed with members of the custodial staff? Why or why not?

- Should the principal help clean up the school? Why or why not?

- Do you consider cleaning up the school a form of punishment? Why?

- Are there any students who should be excused from the after-school clean up? Who and why?

- What other solution could there be to this problem?

- Imagine you are one of the custodians. How do you feel about the cleanliness of the school?

- How might a custodian react to the principal's plan?

- What might parents do in response to the principal's plan? Why?

Step 5: A round of applause

Let your actors sit down, and have the class give them a round of applause.

Step 6: Write or scribe a prompt response

Ask your students to read the original prompt again. If you turned off the projector or removed the prompt, make it available again for everyone to view. This is important because during the assessment test the students will be looking at a few sentences on a page, not a live enactment.

If you will be scribing a response with your students, have them gather around the easel and chart pad. Use the ideas from your discussion to draft the opening of your response. Refer to pages 23–26 for how to proceed from the beginning to the middle to the end of the scribed response. If students are writing on their own, have them begin working while their ideas are fresh in their minds.

The letter format includes the name and address of the school, the date, a greeting punctuated by a comma, and a signature.

The enactment often sparks enthusiasm and improves writing, because students get excited about sharing and formulating opinions. Persuasive prompts are the perfect opportunity for students to develop the skills to present their opinion, to listen to an opposing opinion, and not to end up in an argument. It is helpful for many students to learn how to do this if they are required to take a stance contrary to what they actually believe. When children collect ideas to support a contrasting

Name of School
Address
Town, State Zip Code

Date

Dear _____ ,

_____

_____

_____

_____

_____

_____

_____

Sincerely,

_____

(Signature)

opinion, it sets the stage for seeing both sides of a topic, which is important in team building and conflict resolution situations.

Step 7: Self-edit the response

Once the written responses are finished, it is time for students to edit them. If you have scribed a response, you can self-edit as a group. If students have written on their own, the self-editing can be done a number of ways, all of which begin with the Standing Ovation Checklist for Persuasive Prompts. See page 93 and the CD-ROM for a reproducible handout of the checklist; see page 37 for more on coding written responses. The checklist for persuasive prompts has several elements that do not appear on other versions of the checklist. Elements unique to this checklist are explained on pages 94–95.

- You may ask students to code their stories to the checklist.
- You may have students trade with a partner and code each other's responses. It is often easier for students to edit someone else's work than their own.

- You may have students work in pairs or groups using the appropriate Standing Ovation Checklist Playing Cards (see pages 47–52).

Once a student's response is coded, he or she should revise the piece, adding any missing elements. Students may also embellish ideas or add details or entirely new support reasons. If you are practicing for the test, remind your students that they must finish writing during a specific amount of time. Once they begin the test, they should not attempt to erase an entire page or write a new "improved" draft, because they may run out of time. For other assignments during the year, you may want to require clean new second drafts.

If students are struggling with how to add a particular element, make sure they know they can seek help from you or another classroom assistant. While students are self-editing, walk among them, checking in about their progress and comfort with the writing prompt and checklist. You may call a few students together for a mini-lesson on a common need.

The Standing Ovation Checklist

For Persuasive Prompts

	Yes	No
1. The response uses the format of a letter (header, date, greeting, closing).		
2. The response is written to the audience described in the prompt.		
3. The opening includes a hook, a statement of your position, and a summary of your supporting reasons.		
4. The response includes at least three persuasive reasons to support your position.		
5. Each reason is supported by details.		
6. The reasons are addressed in the same order as presented in the opening.		
7. The response includes at least three transitional words.		
8. The response acknowledges another point of view in one or two sentences.		
9. The closing makes a plea to the reader to agree with you.		
10. At least two of the three forms of ending punctuation are included in the response: period (.), question mark (?), and exclamation point (!).		
11. The response contains broad and accurate vocabulary.		
12. The response includes action and rich details.		
13. The response stays on the topic of the prompt.		
14. Each new paragraph is indented.		
15. The response has been written neatly.		
16.		
17.		

Elements Unique to the Persuasive Prompt Checklist

Since persuasive writing involves skills that other forms of writing do not, the checklist for persuasive writing has several unique elements, and elements from other lists that are not applicable have been omitted.

1. The response uses the format of a letter.

The parts of a letter include a header with the return address, the date, a greeting, and a closing with the student's signature. Students should use the name of your school along with the city and state rather than their own home address. This is especially important if you plan to mail students' letters (see page 96).

2. The response is written to the audience described in the prompt.

Using the school example on page 89, the audience is the school principal. Students should put that person's title in the greeting of the letter ("Dear Principal"). When students take assessments, their responses are read and scored by someone the students do not know and will never meet, but they should still address their responses to the audience described in the prompt.

3. The opening includes a hook, a statement of your position, and a summary of your supporting reasons.

The opening of a persuasive essay needs to get the reader's attention with a good hook, such as a quotation, a fact, or creatively stating the point of view. The hook causes the reader to want to know more about the student's point of view and why he or she has

that perspective. The opening should then clearly summarize the issue and the writer's point of view on the issue. Finally, it should contain the three or more reasons the writer will use to defend or support the point of view. Here's an example of a strong opening to a student essay written by a sixth grader.

> Moffitt Intermediate School
> 1234 Cherry Tree Road
> Sassville, MN, USA 54321
>
> March 1, 2010
>
> Dear Principal Franks,
>
> Wow, this school is a mess! I know you feel the same way, but I am not sure that spending half an hour a week working with a custodian is the solution. First, we have winning teams and our players can't miss games to clean the halls. Second, we can identify the students who make the mess. Third, it would cramp my style. Please consider the three reasons why I feel this way and then reconsider your plan. Although we don't know each other very well because I don't get in trouble too often, I believe that you are a fair principal and will see my point of view, which I will explain below.

4. The response includes at least three persuasive reasons to support your position.

Reasons should directly support the writer's perspective, and they should persuade by taking into account the audience's point of view. Consider the following examples from the same essay:

First, this season we have a few winning teams. If the members of the teams are late getting to practice or to their games because they have to clean the hallways, that will hurt our school's morale. And if those kids are let off the hook and don't have to clean because they are on those teams, that would send the wrong message to the other students.

Next, we have great technology in our school we could use to our advantage. Why should all of the students have to work for half an hour when we can identify the students causing the mess? You can use the security cameras to record the hallways and exits. Then you will catch the culprits. I volunteer to help identify the students.

5. Each reason is supported by details.

The details may be further explanation, facts, examples, or real experiences. Look again at the example above to see how a student can elaborate on reasons with detail.

6. The reasons are addressed in the same order as presented in the opening.

The opening of the letter is like a map that shows how the body of the letter will read, so it's important that the reasons are addressed in the same order in the body as they are introduced in the opening.

7. The response includes at least three transitional words.

Transition words help readers navigate the response. Often, the first word or phrase in a paragraph is a transition word. Basic choices include *first, next, then, in conclusion, finally,* and *most important.* These words signal the progress of events or a sequence of reasons. Sometimes the words signal a level of importance for the reasons

and details. Other times they signal steps in a process or procedure.

8. The response acknowledges another point of view in one or two sentences.

Students in grades 3–8 may not need to refute opposing viewpoints, but simply acknowledge another perspective. The ability to see both (or multiple) sides of a situation is an advanced skill, showing that the writer understands the issue and is open to ideas. It can help assure readers who hold an opposing viewpoint that the writer has at least considered their position.

An alternative point of view is to ask the custodians for a solution. Have you done that already? They may not want the kids tagging along. Before imposing your plan on us, please look at it again.

9. The closing makes a plea to the reader to agree with you.

The goal of persuasive writing is, of course, to get the reader to agree with you. It's not enough for a writer to state what he or she feels and why; the writer needs to appeal directly to the reader. Consider the questions: Who is the reader? Why should the reader see it my way? Here is a closing that appeals to the reader:

In conclusion, Principal Franks, I ask that you address the mess in the school but reconsider your solution. I would be happy to spend half an hour in your office talking about other solutions. (Yikes, I think I just volunteered to go to the principal's office!) I am on your side and know that as a team we can make the school less of a mess.

Sincerely,
Ivy Star

Delivering Letters

To make persuasive letter-writing a more authentic experience for students, mail their letters. Read the letters first to make sure they are appropriate. Send the letters at least 6 to 8 weeks before the end of the school year so the reader has time to respond. For security and confidentially reasons, your contact address should be the school's mailing address, not students' home addresses. Even if you think each student will receive a response, don't promise what you can't guarantee.

It may be easier and quicker to send letters via email. As with regular mail, be vigilant about security and confidentiality. Use your own school account rather than personal student accounts. However, sometimes a handwritten letter—or a bundle of handwritten letters—can be more effective than email. A teacher in Hope's district compiled letters from her students into a spiral bound booklet. She mailed those handwritten letters to a popular TV personality. Four months later, the teacher and principal received a phone call and an email. Their persuasive letters had convinced this celebrity to make a generous donation to the cause the students had written about. The students learned about the power of persuasive writing and how they could make a difference in someone's life as they were told how much of a positive impact their words had on the reader.

Chapter 11
The Poetry Prompt

Poetry prompts provide a piece of poetry for students to respond to. After students read the poem (for some state assessments, the proctor also reads the poem aloud), they are expected to demonstrate their comprehension of the poem by responding to specific questions provided in the prompt. Students should not only summarize the main idea of the poem but also analyze it by making a personal (text-to-self, text-to-text, or text-to-world) connection.

Make sure students know they are not writing a poem, but responding to a poem. Responses should include all the elements on the Standing Ovation Checklist for Poetry Prompts, which contains several elements not included on checklists for other prompts. See page 101.

Poetry Prompt Sources

For most of the year, you can use the poetry prompts provided in Part 4 of this book, on pages 148–157, or you can find your own. Make finding poems part of your classroom activity. The more students are engaged in the prompts themselves, the more readily they'll engage in the writing process.

You can find poems in poetry books, including anthologies and readers. You can also find them on greeting cards, in magazines, and on the Web. Song lyrics can make great poetry prompts if they are age- and content-appropriate. Invite students to write poems to share with the class. **Please note that in order to legally reproduce poems or song lyrics, you will need to secure permission from the publishers.** However, it is fine to look at a Web site or other published source together without copying it.

If your students will be responding to poetry prompts on their assessment test, you will eventually want to start using prompts that more accurately reflect those they'll find on the test. You may even be able to find poetry prompts used in previous tests. See pages 44–45.

Enacting the Prompt

When preparing for the enactment process with a poetry prompt, be sure your students understand what kind of writing will be expected: a summary and analysis of the poem in which they make a personal connection. The enactment process is discussed in greater detail in chapter 2.

See It

They Pick Me Last in Gym Class*
by Tammy Scott

On Monday we played soccer and I even scored a goal.
Why should it really matter that I ran into the pole?

On Tuesday we played run and tag and I thought I did well.
It's not my fault my shoe untied or that I tripped and fell.

On Wednesday it was kickball and the team I played for won.
I made it once to first base, but I didn't score a run.

On Thursday we chose tug of war. I pulled with all my might.
Who knew the rope was slippery and I wasn't holding tight?

On Friday we played baseball and I took a real big swing.
I missed the ball and I struck out. It must not be my thing.

They pick me last in gym class and I really don't know why.
I may not be athletic, but at least I always try.

In "They Pick Me Last in Gym Class," poet Tammy Scott talks about the frustration of not doing as well as she'd like in gym class. At one time or another, most of us have worked hard to do something that was difficult for us. Write a composition about continuing to try and not giving up. In your composition be sure to:

- describe what you were trying to do
- explain why you didn't give up
- analyze what you could do to help you accomplish your goal

Step 1: View the prompt

Show your students the prompt, preferably by hanging a large poster or projecting the poem and related questions. Be sure everyone can see the prompt clearly, and distribute a copy of the poem to each student as well (if you have permission). Read the prompt aloud, including the writing task at the end of the poem, then give your students a couple minutes to read it silently to themselves and think about it. On the left side of this page is an example of a poetry prompt.

Step 2: Discuss the prompt

After two minutes, have a class discussion in which students share their thoughts about the poem and what they might include in their responses. This is a brainstorming session, so explain that there are no right or wrong answers and all ideas are valued. It should be a lively, nonjudgmental discussion. The point is to get students thinking critically and creatively about the prompt. They should think about the personal connection they can make to the poem and the writing task at the end.

Step 3: Enact the prompt

Ask for volunteers from the class to enact the prompt. Depending on the level of confidence and skill in your class, you may have them simply create a frozen image that they come up with, mime a simple action, or act out a full scene including dialogue. They should become the characters in the poem, and maybe even the props, if appropriate. For example, students enacting "They Pick Me Last in Gym Class" might decide to enact the activities the narrator does on each day of the week, or the choosing of teams with one student being picked last.

Remind the other students to actively observe the enactment and think about what is happening in the picture. They participate as active members of the audience.

Step 4: Discuss the enactment

While students are enacting the scene, use the checklist to guide a discussion about the early elements in the response, including the hook, the main idea of the poem, and ways students might find personal connections to the poem. Whether you will scribe a story as a group or students will write on their own, you will want to take notes on the ideas generated, either on a white board or chalk board or somewhere else.

Ask students, "If you were a character in this poem, how would you feel? How would you describe your feelings to a friend?" To spark lively and relevant student participation, continue asking your students questions that pertain to the poem and the bullet points in the writing task. Depending on how your discussion goes, actors may change positions, speak as if in character, and evolve the scene. This shows your students how a poetry response can evolve and how several responses can come from one prompt.

Here is a list of general discussion questions to use with most poetry prompts:

- What is the title of the poem?
- Who is the author of the poem?
- Who are the characters in the poem?
- How do the characters know each other?
- What is the setting (time and location) of the scene?
- What are the characters doing? What problem or situation are the characters facing or involved in?

Be It

- Why are the characters there? Why are they in this situation?

You may want to ask more specific questions about the individual prompt you are using, in particular about how students can make a connection to the poem (similar situations they've been in, etc.). A good way to start is by asking if any of the students have any experience with the topic of the poem or similar topics. Go further by asking students what feelings their experience evoked in them or might evoke.

For the poem "They Pick Me Last in Gym Class," you might ask questions like the following to get students thinking about what is going on in the poem and relating it to their own personal experiences. It may only take one or two questions to get your class talking about the prompt and making their own text-to-self, text-to-text, or text-to-world connections.

- Who tries hard in this poem? What does that person try to do?
- What seems to go wrong each day of the week?
- Why do you think the person keeps trying?

- Why is the person picked last?
- How do the other kids in the gym class feel about the main character in the poem?
- What is the person's goal?
- When did you have to try hard in gym class or another class?
- How did you feel?
- Was there a time you didn't give up?
- When did you keep trying to do something that was difficult?
- Why did you keep trying?
- Did you accomplish your goal?
- Why or why not?

Step 5: A round of applause

Let your actors sit down, and have the class give them a round of applause.

Step 6: Write or scribe a prompt response

Ask your students to read the original poem again. If you turned off the projector or removed the prompt, make it available again for everyone to view. This is important because during the assessment test the students will be looking at a few sentences on a page, not a live enactment.

If you will be scribing a response with your students, have them gather around the easel and chart pad. Use the ideas from your discussion to draft the opening of your response. Refer to pages 23–26 for how to proceed from the beginning to the middle to the end of the scribed response. If students are writing on their own, have them begin working while ideas are fresh in their minds.

Step 7: Self-edit the response

Once the written responses are finished, it is time for students to edit them. If you have scribed a response, you can self-edit as a group. If students have written on their own, the self-editing can be done a number of ways, all of which begin with the Standing Ovation Checklist for Poetry Prompts. See page 101 and the CD-ROM for a reproducible handout of the checklist; see page 37 for more on coding written responses. The checklist for poetry prompts has several elements that do not appear on other versions of the checklist (though it has the same elements as the checklist for quote or adage prompts). Elements unique to this checklist are explained on pages 102–103.

- You may ask students to code their stories to the checklist.
- You may have students trade with a partner and code each other's responses. It is often easier for students to edit someone else's work than their own.
- You may have students work in pairs or groups using the appropriate Standing Ovation Checklist Playing Cards (see pages 47–52).

Once a student's response is coded, he or she should revise the piece, adding any missing elements. Students may also embellish ideas or add entirely new ones. If you are practicing for the test, encourage them not to add too much or write entirely new drafts, because they may run out of time. But for other assignments during the year, you may want to require clean new second drafts.

If students are struggling with how to add a particular element, make sure they know they can seek help from you or another classroom assistant. While students are self-editing, walk among them, checking in about their progress and comfort with the writing prompt and checklist. You may call a few students together for a mini-lesson on a common need.

The Standing Ovation Checklist

For Poetry Prompts

	Yes	No
1. The opening includes a hook, the title of the poem, and the author's name.		
2. The response draws a connection between the poem's main idea and your personal experience.		
3. The response includes at least two of the three forms of ending punctuation: period (.), question mark (?), and exclamation point (!).		
4. The response contains broad and accurate vocabulary.		
5. The response includes action and rich details.		
6. The response is written in a logical sequence and uses transitional words.		
7. Key ideas are developed with details and direct connections to the poem.		
8. The response is written for an audience who does not know you.		
9. The response concludes with a strong ending.		
10. The response uses proper grammar and word usage.		
11. The response stays on the topic of the prompt.		
12. Each new paragraph is indented.		
13. The response has been written neatly.		
14.		
15.		

Elements Unique to the Poetry Prompt Checklist

Responding to poems involves skills that other forms of writing do not, so the poetry prompt checklist has several unique elements, and elements from other checklists that are not applicable have been omitted. Please refer to chapter 3 for more information on checklist items not discussed on the following pages.

1. The opening includes a hook, the title of the poem, and the author's name.

The hook serves the same purpose in a poetry response as it does in other kinds of writing: to gain the reader's attention. A good way to do this is by setting a scene that shows the writer's personal connection to the poem. After the hook, writers should restate the title and author of the poem to focus their response. Here's a sample opening written by a gifted fourth grader:

> Riding a bike looks much easier than it really is! I remember when I was trying to learn how to keep my balance and ended up falling over and over again. No matter what I did, I would end up on the sidewalk. The poem "They Pick Me Last in Gym Class" by Tammy Scott reminds me of when I was trying to learn to ride my bike.

2. The response draws a connection between the poem's main idea and the writer's personal experience.

To show they understand the meaning of the poem, students should summarize its main idea. They should then make a text-to-self, text-to-text, or text-to-world connection to the poem. This shows they truly understand the poem.

6. The response is written in a logical sequence and uses transitional words.

The response should move logically from a beginning that hooks readers and states the writer's personal connection to the poem; to a middle that develops the connection; to an ending that ties it all together for readers. Transitional words include *first, next, then, more importantly, finally, at last, eventually,* and so on.

7. Key ideas are developed with details and direct connections to the poem.

It's not enough for the writer to simply list ways the poem is related to his or her life. Students should make their connections to the poem explicit and detailed. Notice the direct comparisons made by this writer (this is from the same essay excerpted for checklist item #1):

> The person in the poem is always picked last in gym class because she keeps making mistakes and no one wants her on their team. She keeps trying but just can't do anything right. When I was trying to ride my bike, my friends were always making fun of me and didn't want me to ride with them because I would slow them down. Even though I wanted to give up, I didn't want to sit home while everybody else was having fun. If I didn't learn to ride my bike, I'd be stuck. So I kept trying.

8. The response is written for an audience who does not know the writer.

Writers should assume that the reader does not know them or any of the people or events described in their responses. They should describe important people and events in detail so the reader will not have any questions. Looking again at the same fourth grader's writing sample, the writer demonstrates audience awareness by explaining clearly why she wanted to ride her bike, why it was hard, and how her story ended.

> . . . Even though I wanted to give up, I didn't want to sit home while everybody else was having fun. If I didn't learn to ride my bike, I'd be stuck. So I kept trying.
>
> Well I showed them! It didn't make any difference how many cuts and scratches I had all over my body. I didn't give up. Now I can ride as fast as lightning, and my older brother is going to teach me some tricks. Not only can I ride with my friends, I am the fastest on my block.

9. The response concludes with a strong ending.

The ending gives the reader something to take away from the response, such as a question to ponder, a thought about why the topic of the response or poem is important, or a new idea to think about. Below is the conclusion of the student writing sample. Notice how the writer shifts from her own story to speculating what the poem's narrator might be able to do if she never gives up.

> The person in the poem should never give up. I wish I could talk to her and tell her my story. If she keeps trying, maybe someday she'll be picked for a team. Who knows, maybe she could even end up being captain!

One way to help students connect to poetry is through the use of pop music. Most students don't think of their favorite songs as poems set to music, but that is just what they are. A colleague of ours used the lyrics to "Love Story" by Taylor Swift as an introduction to Shakespeare's Romeo and Juliet. Her students were hooked immediately (and the teacher was actually perceived as cool). Together, they not only enjoyed listening to the song and reading the lyrics, they had made a text-to-text connection between the Romeo and Juliet of the song and the classic Romeo and Juliet. If your students are struggling with poetry prompts, bringing in some pop songs for study is a good way to increase enthusiasm.

Chapter 12
The Quote or Adage Prompt

Quote or adage prompts are similar to poetry prompts. After students read the quote or adage (for some state assessments, the proctor also reads the quote or adage aloud), they are expected to demonstrate their comprehension of the text by responding to specific questions provided in the prompt. Students should not only summarize the main idea of the quote or adage but also analyze it by making a personal connection. That connection can be text-to-self, text-to-text, or text-to-world (see page 20). Responses should include all the elements on the Standing Ovation Checklist for Quote or Adage Prompts, which contains several elements not included on checklists for other prompts (but contains the same elements as the poetry checklists). See page 109.

Responding to a quote or adage prompt generally is more difficult than responding to a poetry prompt because a quote provides less text with which students can connect. There are fewer context clues, and the text is often abstract. A student who doesn't understand the quote will have great trouble responding to the prompt. That's why in many states younger students are assessed using poetry prompts and older students are assessed using quote or adage prompts.

What's the difference between a quote and an adage? A quote is often attributed to a speaker or writer and is frequently used to provoke thoughts from the reader. An adage may be an interesting observation, or practical or ethical guideline that many people believe to be true. A quote may become an adage over time.

Quote or Adage Prompt Sources

For most of the year, you can use the quote or adage prompts provided in Part 4 of this book, on pages 158–167, or you can find your own. Numerous books and Web sites provide quotes and adages to use as prompts, including www.brainyquote.com, www.thinkexist.com, and www.quotationspage.com. Students may be interested in current event quotes, which you can find in news-

paper and magazine articles, entertainment or sports figure interviews, and advertisements. You can also find quotes in historical primary sources and fables. Cultural sayings and expressions are a great source for adages.

Ask students to find quotes or adages, or ask families to send ideas. The more students are engaged in the prompts themselves, the more readily they'll engage in the writing process.

It's a good idea to expose students to plenty of quotes and adages, even beyond using them as writing prompts, in order to help them grow more familiar with the form and improve at deciphering them. To do this, share perhaps one quote a day or one a week, and talk together about what they mean. Discuss with students how the quotes relate to their lives. Once students are comfortable reading, analyzing, and connecting with quotes and adages, they are ready to move on to enactments.

Enacting the Prompt

When preparing for the enactment process with a quote or adage prompt, be sure your students understand what kind of writing will be expected: a summary and analysis of the text in which they make a personal connection. The enactment process is discussed in greater detail in chapter 2.

Step 1: View the prompt

Show your students the prompt, preferably by hanging a large poster or projecting the quote and related questions. Be sure everyone can see the prompt clearly, and distribute a copy of the prompt to each student as well. Read the prompt aloud, including the writing task at the end of the quote, then give your students a couple minutes to read it silently to themselves and think about it. An example of a quote prompt is shown on this page.

See It

"A person who never made a mistake never tried anything new."

—*Albert Einstein*

In this quote, Albert Einstein is speaking about the fact that when people try new things, they are likely to make mistakes. Mistakes are part of learning. Write a composition about a time you tried something new and made a mistake. In your composition be sure to:

- describe what you were learning to do

- explain the mistake you made and what you learned from it

- analyze what you did to help you accomplish your goal

Step 2: Discuss the prompt

After two minutes, have a class discussion in which students share their thoughts about the quote and what they might include in their responses. This is a brainstorming session, so explain that there are no right or wrong answers and all ideas are valued. It should be a lively, nonjudgmental discussion. The point is to get students thinking critically and creatively about the prompt. They should think about the personal connection they can make to the quote and the writing task at the end.

Step 3: Enact the prompt

Ask for volunteers from the class to enact the prompt. Depending on the level of confidence and skill in your class, you may have them simply create a frozen image that they come up with, mime a simple action, or act out a full scene including dialogue. They should become the characters in the quote, and maybe even the props, if appropriate.

Students should enact a moment that reflects the meaning or message of the quote. Did they ever experience anything that the quote seems to be talking about? If not, can they imagine such an experience? For example, students enacting the Albert Einstein quote would probably enact a scene in which someone tries something new and fails, such as a science experiment that goes wrong; a missed attempt to shoot a basket; a mistake made when learning to double-dutch with jump ropes; or falling down when learning to ride a bike.

Remind the other students to actively observe the enactment and think about what is happening in the picture. They participate as active members of the audience.

Step 4: Discuss the enactment

While students are enacting the scene, use the checklist to guide a discussion about the early elements in the response, including the hook, the main idea of the quote or adage, and ways students might find personal connections to the quote or adage. Whether you will scribe a story as a group or students will write on their own, you will want to take notes on the ideas generated, either on a white board or chalk board or somewhere else.

Ask students, "What does this quote mean to you?" To spark lively and relevant student participation, continue asking your students questions that pertain to the quote and the bullet points in the writing task. Depending on how your discussion goes, actors may change positions, speak as if in character, and evolve the scene. This shows your students how a quote or adage response can evolve and how several responses can come from one prompt.

Here is a list of general discussion questions to use with most quote or adage prompts:

- To whom is this quote/adage attributed?
- Are you familiar with this person? If so, what do you know about this person?
- Have you ever heard or read this quote/adage before?
- What is the meaning of the quote/adage?
- What experience in your life can be applied to the message of the prompt?
- If you have not had a direct experience related to the meaning of the quote, has someone else in your family or friendship circle had such an experience?

You may want to ask more specific questions about the individual prompt you are using, in particular about how students can make a connection to the quote or adage (similar situations they've been in, etc.). Ask if any of your students have any experience with the topic of the quote or similar topics. Go further by asking students what feelings their experience evoked in them or might evoke.

For the Einstein quote, you might ask students questions like the following to get them thinking about the meaning of the quote and relating it to their own personal experiences. It may only take one or two questions to get your class talking about the prompt and making their own text-to-self, text-to-text, or text-to-world connections.

- Who is Albert Einstein? (It's okay if students don't know who the speaker is, but if they do know, they may be able to gain better insight into the meaning of the quote. State assessments do not require students to know who the speaker is.)

- Why do you think he said this?

- How might this quote be related to his life?

- Have you ever tried something new? What was it?

- Why did you try it?

- Was it easy or hard? Why? Did you make a mistake?

- How long did it take to learn it?

- Did you ever feel discouraged? If so, did you keep trying? Why or why not?

- How did you know you had learned it?

- Did people support you when you made mistakes? How did you know?

- If you had to do it over again and knew how difficult it was, what would you do differently? Why?

- What advice would you give to someone who is trying to learn the same thing?

- What other mistakes have you learned from?

- How does it feel to make mistakes?

- What new thing would you like to try next? Why?

Some of your students may understand the quote but have no personal experience that relates to it. Encourage these students to make text-to-world or text-to-text connections by writing about how the prompt relates to someone they know, read about, or saw in a movie or on TV.

Step 5: A round of applause

Let your actors sit down, and have the class give them a round of applause.

Step 6: Write or scribe a prompt response

Ask your students to read the original prompt again. If you turned off the projector or removed the prompt, make it available again for everyone to view. This is important because during the assessment test the students will be looking at a few sentences on a page, not a live enactment.

If you will be scribing a response with your students, have them gather around the easel and chart pad. Use the ideas from your discussion to draft the opening of your response. Refer to pages 23–26 for how to proceed from the beginning to the middle to the end of the scribed response. If students are writing on their own, have them begin working while ideas are fresh in their minds.

Step 7: Self-edit the response

Once the written responses are finished, it is time for students to edit them. If you have scribed a response, you can self-edit as a group. If students have written on their own, the self-editing can be done a number of ways, all of which begin with the Standing Ovation Checklist for Quote or Adage Prompts. See page 109 and the CD-ROM for a reproducible handout of the checklist; see page 37 for more on coding written responses.

The checklist for quote or adage prompts has several elements that do not appear on other versions of the checklist, but its elements are identical to those found on the checklist for poetry prompts. For an explanation of elements unique to the quote or adage checklist, see the explanation for the poetry checklist on pages 102–103.

- You may ask students to code their stories to the checklist.
- You may have students trade with a partner and code each other's responses. It is often easier for students to edit someone else's work than their own.
- You may have students work in pairs or groups using the appropriate Standing Ovation Checklist Playing Cards (see pages 47–52).

Once a student's response is coded, he or she should revise the piece, adding any missing elements. Students may also embellish ideas or add entirely new ones. If you are practicing for the test, encourage them not to add too much or write entirely new drafts, because they may run out of time. But for other assignments during the year, you may want to require clean new second drafts.

If students are struggling with how to add a particular element, make sure they know they can seek help from you or another classroom assistant. While students are self-editing, walk among them, checking in about their progress and comfort with the writing prompt and checklist. You may call a few students together for a mini-lesson on a common need.

The Standing Ovation Checklist

For Quote or Adage Prompts

	Yes	No
1. The opening includes a hook, the title of the quote or adage, and the author's name.		
2. The response draws a connection between the main idea of the quote or adage and your personal experience.		
3. The response includes at least two of the three forms of ending punctuation: period (.), question mark (?), and exclamation point (!).		
4. The response contains broad and accurate vocabulary.		
5. The response includes action and rich details.		
6. The response is written in a logical sequence.		
7. Key ideas are developed with details and direct connections to the quote or adage.		
8. The response is written for an audience who does not know you.		
9. The response concludes with a strong ending.		
10. The response uses proper grammar and word usage.		
11. The response stays on the topic of the prompt.		
12. Each new paragraph is indented.		
13. The response has been written neatly.		
14.		
15.		

Chapter 13
Cross-Curricular Connections

While the enactment process is primarily a means of improving student writing, it is a flexible tool that can be used in most curricular areas. If you teach multiple subjects to your students, this is an effective way to increase efficiency: students work on their writing skills at the same time they focus on new content areas. You can also teach test prep skills and strategies for both subjects at the same time. With all that teachers are responsible for, the benefits of such a time saver are obvious.

In addition to saving time, the enactment process is an effective way to teach content because students are actively learning. Just as enacting a prompt helps students engage more directly with a writing task, enacting an assignment in a content area helps students engage with that content. For that reason, the enactment process is also a great tool for teachers of single content areas—say a middle school history teacher. Imagine enacting a scene from the first Olympic games or Rosa Parks's refusal to give up her seat on an Alabama bus in 1955.

A Thematic Approach

Using the enactment process across the curriculum helps drive home to students that when they write in subject areas other than English language arts, the requirements and expectations are the same. Good writing is a life skill and should not be confined to English class and writing tests. Likewise, successful writing—whether on class assignments, on the state assessment, or outside school entirely—is built from materials and ideas that come from all classes. When students include content-area details in their writing, their writing is stronger. It reflects confidence, higher order thinking skills, and a wide knowledge base. Helping students do this is a shared responsibility of all teaching staff, from math to music, gym to geography.

We cannot assume that students understand that good writing skills need to be applied to all writing tasks. We learned this the hard way when, following the math section of the state assessment, we chatted with our students about how they felt they did. They told us the open-ended math questions were the most difficult. When we asked them if they used the elements of good writing they'd learned in language arts in their responses, a look of horror crossed their faces. One precocious young man, and one of our best writers, exclaimed, "You mean we have to write like that in math, too?" The room went silent. We asked how many students included punctuation and the elements of good writing in their responses, and not one student raised a hand.

As teachers, it is our responsibility to model and reinforce good writing in every subject so that good writing becomes habit. One way to do this is through thematic assignments, in which one subject or idea is the basis for instruction in several content areas. For example, using lemonade as a theme and starting with the lemonade picture prompt featured in chapter 2, Hope designed a cross-curricular unit for the third through fifth graders she was working with:

- To teach vocabulary skills, she borrowed a cardboard lemonade stand to use as a prop. This was helpful for students who had no prior knowledge of lemonade sales, especially English language learners, who learned vocabulary and information needed to proceed.

- To teach physical education, she invited the PE teacher to juggle lemons for the class. This gave students a sneak preview of what they would be learning later in the school year because hand-eye coordination activities such as cup stacking and juggling were part of the PE curriculum.

- To teach reading comprehension, she used lemonade stories for read aloud time.

- To teach visual arts, she asked the art teacher to incorporate yellow paint and crayons into her still life art lessons.

- To teach home economics, she shared recipes for lemonade, lemon bars, and lemon muffins. These were compiled into a lemon recipe book that was shared with all the classes.

- To teach math, she created lemonade-based math word problems.

- To teach science, she presented lessons about the life cycle of a lemon tree.

If you teach all subjects to one class, a thematic unit is easy enough to create and execute, since you are in control of all content. If you are an English teacher whose students learn other subjects from other teachers, collaborating with colleagues on a thematic unit is a great way to build camaraderie. Students find thematic learning refreshing and fun, and their learning can go so much deeper when subject matter is developed across the curriculum. In all content areas, the enactment process can bring facts to life and clarify information. Students then can demonstrate their deeper understanding in their written responses.

Director's Note

Even without doing a curriculum-wide themed unit, English teachers can still teach students the valuable lesson that good writing applies to all subject areas. One way to do this is to assign a writing prompt that reviews previously mastered material from another subject, such as math, science, or social studies. 🎭

One thematic unit we've had success with is "American Icon," based on the popular TV show *American Idol*. After showing students a finale episode of the show, we assigned a speculative writing assignment in which students wrote about how it would feel to win the show and how life would change for them. We also had students write about what it would be like if they won but then lost their voice. For math, students wrote about how they'd spend their prize money; for social studies, they mapped out a concert tour; and for character education, they wrote about talking with other contestants after they are announced as the winner. It's easy to come up with ideas for your class in all subject areas.

Writing Prompts for Content Areas

The following section provides writing prompts for specific content areas. Feel free to use these ideas as they are or as a springboard to develop your own prompt ideas.

Math writing prompts

Write a story from a graph.

Display a graph as a writing prompt. Have a preliminary discussion with your students about what the graph says, and then have them do an enactment about it and write a response. You can have them write speculative responses or relate the graph to their own lives as they would with a poetry or quote/adage response.

Here is a sample graph and assignment:

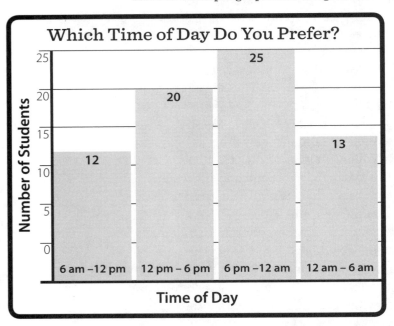

This graph depicts information about the time of day preferred by seventy students. Students' written responses may be about favorite activities done during specific time frames, why they agree or don't agree with the data, or which time of day is their favorite and why. They must include data from the graph in their story.

Students might enact the graph itself by standing in lines to represent each bar on the graph or enact the different activities that take place during each time frame referenced on the graph. You may also reverse this activity by asking students to write their story first and then create a graph from the information created.

A world with no numbers

Choose one of the following scenarios, read it to your students, and ask for volunteers to enact the scenario.

- Two people buy groceries in a world with no numbers.
- Friends go to the movies in a world with no numbers.
- You are looking for a friend's home you've never visited in a world with no numbers.

After the enactment, have students write a speculative response. This activity makes students explore the concept of numeration systems and their importance and relevance in everyday life. Without being able to use numbers, the students in the enactment would not know how much the groceries would cost, the friends would show up at different times for the movie, and it certainly would be difficult to find a house without an address. This prompt really gets the creative juices flowing as students speculate what a numberless world would be like.

Fund-raising run

Read the following scenario to students: "Your club raised $500 to improve your school. How did you raise the money? What is your plan for improving the school? Include a detailed budget in your answer."

After a preliminary discussion, ask for volunteers to enact the fund-raising efforts or the improvement plan, then have students write a story that explains how they raised the money and how they would use it to fix the school. Their stories must demonstrate the use of a budget.

A car of the future

As a group or individually, have students design and draw a picture of a car of the future. Establish the features and price of the car, then ask for volunteers to enact a commercial for it. Next, have students write a persuasive essay in which they try to convince readers to buy the car. They must include the price and accurate monthly payments they have calculated including tax and interest. (You can get information on interest rates from a bank Web site.)

New form of money

Your country is changing over to a new form of currency. Have your students invent this new money. They must actually create the money and assign worth to different denominations. They can draw pieces of the money, describe it in writing, or represent it physically with beans or stones or something else. Have students enact the first monetary transaction using their money. Have them determine the price of something and pay for it with their money. Make sure the actors have to make and count change. Finally, have students write a news story about where the new money was used for the first time, why it was used, by whom it was used, and people's reactions to using this new form of money. Were there any problems getting used to the new money? There are lots of possibilities for this writing response.

Funny money

Tell students they have won a contest and the prize is a sum of money (decide how much you want it to be). If you want, fill envelopes with fake money and deliver it to students. You can have students do individual or group enactments to show how they would use their money, or have students pool their money, calculate the total, and do an enactment showing how they'd use the group prize. Then have students write a story or press release explaining in detail how they'd use the money (individual or class total).

Equation station

Provide your students with an equation appropriate to their grade level, then have students enact the number sentence. For example, given the number sentence $(27 + 54) \times 2 = 162$, students could enact making lunches for the class: 27 sandwiches and 54 cookies. Then they could enact a second class coming to lunch to bring the total to 162 lunch items made. The students then write a story that uses the number sentence.

Science writing prompts

The forensic science writing prompt

Prior to your class coming in, stage a crime scene in your classroom (turn some desks over, throw papers on the floor, open a window, etc.) and have your students write a story about what they think happened. They should use scientific investigation skills and knowledge to construct a reasonably feasible idea. (Older students may have seen the *CSI: Crime Scene Investigation* television shows, which you can use to bring extra excitement to the assignment.)

Cloud formations

Have students look at pictures of different types of clouds, or take them outside to look at clouds. How do different kinds of clouds affect the weather? Imagine being in one of those clouds, or, better yet, being one. Next have students enact different types of clouds and write stories about living on a particular type of cloud. They could also write stories from the perspective of a cloud formation. Be sure they use their knowledge about the science of clouds to inform their stories.

Life cycles

Ask for volunteers to enact the life cycle of an organism you're studying. Next, remove one step of the life cycle and enact it again. How would this missing step impact the organism? Have students write a speculative response that explores what would happen.

Food chains

Ask for volunteers to enact a food chain or food web from a biome you're studying. Next, remove one step of the food chain and enact it again. How would this missing step impact the food chain? Have students write a speculative response that explores what would happen.

Rain, rain, go away!

If you are studying weather or the water cycle, have students enact a rainy day. Then have them enact a drought. Have them enact what would happen if it rained every day for a year in your town. Have students write a speculative response that explores what would happen if it rained every day or were sunny every day for a year. Make sure to include the environmental impact of the weather.

Social studies prompts

Cave painting

If you are studying early human life, have students enact ancient humans creating a cave painting. Have all your students help create a cave painting on butcher paper. What do the symbols mean? What does the painting say? Have students write a response that answers these questions.

Hieroglyphics story

Ask for volunteers to enact finding a piece of papyrus containing hieroglyphics, then have students write a story about where it was found and what message it conveys.

Map story

Project a map on the wall (you can use one from a source you're studying or make your own) to use as a prompt. As a group, discuss what the map shows and ask for volunteers to enact a story that takes place in the area represented. Have students write a story (speculative response) about what happens before, after, or during the enacted part.

Songs about cities around the world

Listen to songs about specific places (cities, towns, countries, etc.), such as "New York, New York," "Chicago," "I Love Paris," "I Left My Heart in San Francisco," "Istanbul (Not Constantinople)," "Graceland," "Georgia on My Mind," "Galway Bay," or others. You might want to look at the lyrics on a Web site or by projecting a CD insert. (Important: you will need to secure permission to reproduce the lyrics in any way.)

Next, use maps or a globe to find the locations and ask for volunteers to enact an imaginary visit. For written responses, you can have students write about how the song makes them feel about the location (for instance would they like to go there?). You can also have them write a story about going there. How would they get there? Who would they see there? What would they do? Other ideas include having students draw their own maps or create travel brochures for the location.

Visual arts prompts

Many important moments in history have been captured in paintings and photographs, and some have become icons of our culture. Examples include Emanuel Leutze's painting "Washington Crossing the Delaware," Alfred Eisenstead's photograph "V-J Day in Times Square" (the kissing sailor) that was published in Life magazine in 1945, and "The Coronation of Napoleon" by Jacques-Louis David. Choose one or more of these paintings or photographs as relevant to an era you are studying to discuss as a class. Ask for volunteers to enact the image, then have your students write about the details they see in the image. You might also want to have them draw or paint their own images about the same moment or another moment from your studies. For a fun twist, listen to the song "Kodachrome" by Paul Simon, which talks about capturing the vibrancy of rich colors and images in photography. It can help motivate students to include such details in their art *and* writing.

Music prompts

Music can be a wonderful catalyst for student writing. While the following prompts do not teach music curriculum, they use music as speculative, persuasive, poetry, or quote/adage prompts. In each case, project a Web page or CD insert so you can look at the lyrics together as you listen to the song. (Do not reproduce the lyrics unless you get permission from the music company that holds the rights.) Make sure all lyrics are appropriate for your students before you use them. Students will have a lot of fun enacting these songs.

Song: "Seasons of Love" by the cast of Rent

This song is good for math and SEL lessons. Here are some suggestions:

- Calculate how many lunches your students will eat in a year.
- Calculate how many times they will brush their teeth in a year.
- Calculate how many spelling tests they will take in a year.
- Write about what is meant by a season of love.

Song: "Dancing in the Street" by Mick Jagger and David Bowie

You may prefer the original version by Martha and the Vandellas. This song can be used for social studies. Here are some suggestions:

- Write a story located in one of the cities mentioned in the song.
- Write a story about why people are dancing in the street and not inside.
- Write a story about how dancing is different in different cultures.

Song: "Unwritten" by Natasha Beddingfield

This song is good for SEL lessons. Here are some suggestions:

- Write a story explaining how your life is an unwritten book.
- Write a story about how you would live your life if you knew the ending now.
- Write a story about becoming a famous author.

Song: "The Lion Sleeps Tonight" by the Tokens

This song is good for science and social studies lessons. Here are some suggestions:

- Write a story with a lion as a central character.
- Write a story about why the lion is considered the king of the jungle.
- Write a story about the lion's role in the jungle's food chain.

Song: "Puff the Magic Dragon" by Peter, Paul and Mary

This song is good for science and social studies lessons. Here are some suggestions:

- Write a story about Puff living somewhere in the city rather than by the sea.
- Write a persuasive letter telling people not to be afraid of Puff.
- Rewrite the lyrics so Puff is an angry dragon.

Song: "Sesame Street Theme Song"

This song is great for social studies lessons. Here are some suggestions:

- Enact a new episode of Sesame Street and write about it. Include dialogue for characters.
- Enact the song using the name of a different street and write about what that street would be like.
- Write a story about how to actually get to Sesame Street.
- Create a map of how to get to Sesame Street.
- Create a new puppet for Sesame Street and write about its role on the show.

Song: "Thriller" by Michael Jackson

This song is great for language arts responses. If possible, show the video, too. Here are some suggestions:

- Write about why monster stories are so popular.
- Write about what scares you.

This is a wonderful song to use to infuse visual arts by making simple costumes. Face painting is hypoallergenic and can add a fun and spooky element.

Song: "Monster Mash" by Bobby Pickett

- Write a story about a party where all the guests are monsters.

Physical education prompts

New rules

Someone changed the rules in your students' favorite game without telling them. Have students discuss, enact the game, and write a speculative response about what would happen.

No rules

This time the rules to a favorite game are eliminated. Have students discuss, enact, and write about what it would be like to play the game without rules, referees, or umpires.

Technology writing prompts

Technology education is no longer a nice bonus for our students; the way technology has become a part of business and everyday life, it's necessary.

Fortunately, it's easy to incorporate technology into the enactment process for any writing assignment. Here are a few examples:

- Use a digital camera to capture the enactment, then upload it to a computer and project it on the wall or print it.
- Create enactment slide shows, which you can publish digitally or in hard copy form.
- Post enactment photos and writing samples on a class Web site or blog.
- Have students give readings of their written responses and post them as podcasts.
- Have students download music or images to accompany enactments or writing assignments. Student essays posted on the class blog or recorded as podcasts can be edited and embellished with images and music.
- Invite families to comment on writing assignments, photos, or podcasts on your class blog or Web site, giving students a taste of what it's like to write for a real audience.
- Use email or Web site contact forms to write to authors, public officials, or others. Students can send persuasive responses, fan mail, or research questions.

Including technology in your writing prompts helps improve students' technological literacy and opens windows to cross the school yard and reach around the globe.

Part 4

Ready-to-Use
Writing Prompts

Picture Prompts, pages 118–127

Speculative Prompts, pages 128–137

Persuasive Prompts, pages 138–147

Poetry Prompts, pages 148–157

Quote or Adage Prompts, pages 158–167

Themed Prompt Sets, pages 168–177

What's in the Box?

A picture tells a story.
Write a story that brings this picture to life.

What's in the Box?

Step 1: Show the prompt

A picture tells a story.
Write a story that brings this picture to life.

Step 2: Discuss the prompt

Have a class discussion about what students see in the picture. Ask, "If this picture could talk, who would be speaking and what would we hear?" Other brainstorming questions include:

- Who might be sending the package?
- Who is receiving the package?
- Why has the package been sent?
- What could be in the box?
- Who sends packages and why?
- Where is the location of the scene?
- When is the package being delivered?
- Who is carrying the package and is the person being careful? How can you tell?
- What would happen if the person dropped the package?
- Is the package heavy or light? How can you tell?

Step 3: Enact the prompt

Here are suggestions for how students could approach the enactment.

1. Have your actors decide what's in the box. One student plays the courier carrying the package and walks to the actors who play the family at a doorway. The adult greets the courier and accepts the package. The kids rip off the paper and act surprised when they look inside the box. Consider using a real box as a prop.

2. As an alternative, have students enact what happens earlier or later in the scene, such as the children in the picture making a phone call to thank a relative for a gift or the family pulling something strange from the box, such as a robot.

Step 4: Discuss the enactment

Consider the following discussion questions.

- What was in the box?
- Was the item intact or broken?
- Who sent the package?
- Why was the package sent?
- Where is a safe place for the delivery person to leave the package if no one is home? Why?
- Does the recipient like what is in the box? How can you tell?
- Was the gift a surprise or something that had been ordered? How can you tell?
- What facial expressions convey surprise?
- What words express surprise?
- Have you or someone in your family ever received a package from a delivery service?
- If so, what was in it? How did it feel to open it? Were you expecting it?

You may want to ask questions that help students develop specific parts of their responses, such as the hook or dialogue.

Step 5: A round of applause

Give your actors a round of applause.

Step 6: Scribe or write a prompt response

Refocus on the prompt rather than the enactment for the written response.

Step 7: Self-edit the response

Use the Standing Ovation Checklist for Picture Prompts.

We're in This Together

A picture tells a story.
Write a story that brings this picture to life.

We're in This Together

Step 1: Show the prompt

A picture tells a story.
Write a story that brings this picture to life.

Step 2: Discuss the prompt

Have a class discussion about what students see in the picture. Ask, "If this picture could talk, who would be speaking and what would we hear?" Other brainstorming questions include:

- What does the word *obedience* mean?
- What might a dog learn to do in obedience school?
- What do dog owners do at obedience school?
- Is there a graduation for the dogs?
- Where are obedience schools located?
- Why do people take their dogs to obedience school?
- What does the dog teacher do?

Step 3: Enact the prompt

Here are suggestions for how students could approach the enactment.

1. Have one to three students act as dog owners entering the obedience school, perhaps discussing why obedience school is needed for this dog. After they enter the class, a student playing the role of class instructor explains what the day's lesson is about and what the owners are to do during this lesson. Act out lessons. This may be humorous or serious. Optional props include a stuffed toy dog that students could hold in their arms or pretend to walk into the class, or a student could play the role of the dog. For the set, students could make a sign that says "Obedience School."

2. Have students enact what happened that led the dog owners to bring their pet to obedience school. This can be a lot of fun with a student playing the role of the dog. The dog could do something mischievous or silly.

3. Have students enact before and after scenarios, in which the dog misbehaves before class and behaves differently after the class. It might be interesting to have students enact a very dramatic change.

Step 4: Discuss the enactment

Consider the following discussion questions.

- Did the dog behave well during obedience class?
- Does the dog like the teacher? Why?
- What was the dog supposed to learn during this class?
- What was the owner supposed to learn during class?
- Who is really being trained, the dog or the person?
- Where is the school located?
- How long is the class?
- Will the dog graduate?
- When does this dog's class meet?
- Does the dog enjoy being at dog obedience school? How can you tell?
- Do any of you have a pet dog?
- Does your dog follow your directions?
- Did your dog go to obedience school or training classes?
- If so, who took the dog to school?

You may want to ask questions that help students develop specific parts of their responses, such as the hook or dialogue.

Step 5: A round of applause

Give your actors a round of applause.

Step 6: Scribe or write a prompt response

Refocus on the prompt rather than the enactment for the written response.

Step 7: Self-edit the response

Use the Standing Ovation Checklist for Picture Prompts.

Ready to Ride

A picture tells a story.
Write a story that brings this picture to life.

Ready to Ride

Step 1: Show the prompt

A picture tells a story.
Write a story that brings this picture to life.

Step 2: Discuss the prompt
Have a class discussion about what students see in the picture. Ask, "If this picture could talk, who would be speaking and what would we hear?" Other brainstorming questions include:

- What is happening in this picture? What will happen next?
- Why do you think that?
- Why do you think requirements or warnings are posted near specific rides?
- What are some other safety warnings you've seen?
- Since the kids had planned to go on the ride together, should they all stay off the ride because one of them wasn't allowed on it?

Step 3: Enact the prompt
Here are suggestions for how students could approach the enactment.

1. Have students enact the scene in the picture, with some playing the role(s) of kids who will get on the ride and some playing the role(s) of kids who will not because they're too short. Tell the actors they have been anxiously awaiting this moment for months, so when they're not allowed to go on the ride it will be very disappointing. Have one student play the role of the ticket taker who will turn away the child or children who do not meet the height requirement. Be sure the students enact how they feel when they realize they will not be allowed on the ride. Students who are allowed on the ride should enact how they feel when their friends are left behind.

2. Have students enact a scene in which the kids try to convince the ticket taker to let them all on, even the kids who do not meet the height requirement.

3. Have students enact alternate endings to the scene, including one where the whole group decides to skip the ride and one where the taller kids leave their friends behind.

Step 4: Discuss the enactment
Consider the following discussion questions.

- Did the kids enjoy the ride?
- What do you think would happen if someone tried to sneak on the ride? What do you think should happen to a person who does so?
- How do you think the ticket collector felt in this scene?
- Do you think there should be age requirements on a ride? Why?
- Is there ever a reason for the height requirement to be waived (ignored)?
- Have you ever been to an amusement park or fair? Where was it and who went with you?
- What was your favorite ride?
- Were you ever frightened on a ride? Why?
- Were there any height requirements or any other warnings that were posted near the ride?

You may want to ask questions that help students develop specific parts of their responses, such as the hook or dialogue.

Step 5: A round of applause
Give your actors a round of applause.

Step 6: Scribe or write a prompt response
Refocus on the prompt rather than the enactment for the written response.

Step 7: Self-edit the response
Use the Standing Ovation Checklist for Picture Prompts.

On My Way

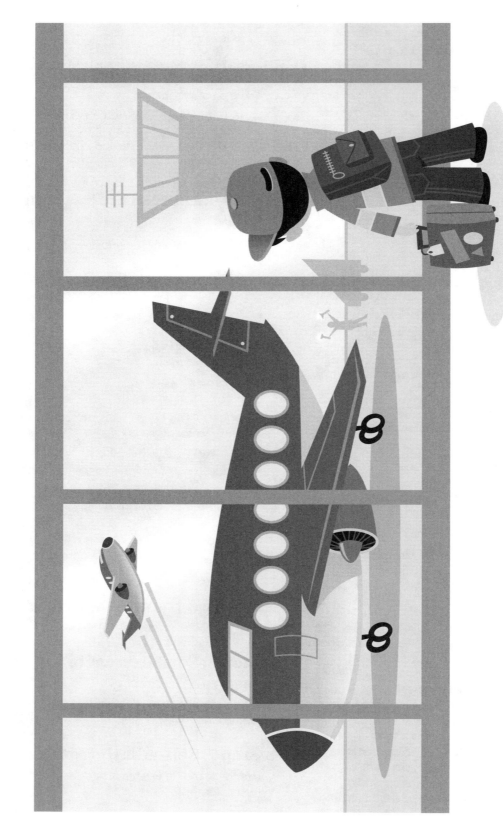

A picture tells a story.
Write a story that brings this picture to life.

On My Way

Step 1: Show the prompt

A picture tells a story.
Write a story that brings this picture to life.

Step 2: Discuss the prompt

Have a class discussion about what students see in the picture. Ask, "If this picture could talk, who would be speaking and what would we hear?" Other brainstorming questions include:

- Why is the boy there? What is he doing?
- What is the boy's name?
- How old is he?
- How does the boy feel?
- What is in his suitcase?
- Does he like to fly?
- Why do you think this boy is looking out the window?

Step 3: Enact the prompt

Here are suggestions for how students could approach the enactment.

1. Put a few desks together to look like a waiting area in an airport. If possible, put them by a window so children can be looking out of the window up at the sky. Next to the desks or chairs, place a few backpacks to simulate the luggage. To continue the scene, you could have the child or children get on the airplane.

2. As a continuation of option #1, or as an alternative, arrange desks to be like rows of seats on an airplane with students seated as passengers. The student who was in the waiting area now boards.

How does the passenger react when he or she gets on the plane alone? How do passengers nearby react when they see a child flying alone? You can also have one pupil be the pilot and others be the crew.

Step 4: Discuss the enactment

Consider the following discussion questions.

- How do you think the child felt?
- Why do you think the child is alone?
- Have you been to an airport?
- Why did you go to the airport?
- Have you flown on a plane?
- Were you excited before your trip? Were you nervous?
- What was your destination? Where did you go?
- Did you travel alone, with friends, or with family?
- Where would you like to go on an airplane trip?
- Would you like to be a pilot or a member of the crew?

You may want to ask questions that help students develop specific parts of their responses, such as the hook or dialogue.

Step 5: A round of applause

Give your actors a round of applause.

Step 6: Scribe or write a prompt response

Refocus on the prompt rather than the enactment for the written response.

Step 7: Self-edit the response

Use the Standing Ovation Checklist for Picture Prompts.

What's So Funny?

A picture tells a story.
Write a story that brings this picture to life.

What's So Funny?

Step 1: Show the prompt

A picture tells a story.
Write a story that brings this picture to life.

Step 2: Discuss the prompt

Have a class discussion about what students see in the picture. Ask, "If this picture could talk, who would be speaking and what would we hear?" Other brainstorming questions include:

- What do you think this family is laughing at?
- Would you like to be one of the people in the car? Which one? Why?
- Which family member do you think is the funniest?
- Where do you think they're going?

Step 3: Enact the prompt

Here are suggestions for how students could approach the enactment.

1. Prior to the enactment, have students decide what is making the family laugh. It may be an actual event that happened to one of the students on the enactment team or a story they make up specifically for the enactment. Or maybe one of the family members told a joke. Set up desks or chairs to look like the inside of a car. Have one or two students take on the role of adults in the front seat and two or three be children in the backseat. For optional props, consider a map, GPS device, or a Frisbee (for the steering wheel). Perhaps the map is the object they're laughing at.

2. To alter the scene slightly, have the kids in the back seat laughing while the adult or adults are upset or impatient. What are some reasons the kids might be laughing while the adults are upset?

Step 4: Discuss the enactment

Consider the following discussion questions.

- What was making the family laugh?
- What are the names of the people in the car?
- Have you ever taken a long family trip in a car? Where did you go? How long did it take to get to your destination?
- Have you ever gotten lost while driving with your family?
- How did it feel when you were lost? How do you think the rest of your family felt?
- How did you finally find your way back to the road you were supposed to be on?
- Do you ever play games in the car during a trip? What are they?
- Do you sing or listen to music while in the car? What type of music or songs does your family like? What type of music or songs do you like?
- Is there a topic that both you and your family find funny? Is there a funny story that makes your family laugh every time they tell it?
- How does laughing make you feel?

You may want to ask questions that help students develop specific parts of their responses, such as the hook or dialogue.

Step 5: A round of applause

Give your actors a round of applause.

Step 6: Scribe or write a prompt response

Refocus on the prompt rather than the enactment for the written response.

Step 7: Self-edit the response

Use the Standing Ovation Checklist for Picture Prompts.

The Surprise Outside

You are at home studying for an important test when your friend calls and says, "You're not going to believe what I found in front of my place!" You run out the door and rush over to your friend's home.

- Write a story about what happens next.
- Be sure to include details in your response.

Use the space below for brainstorming.

The Surprise Outside

Step 1: Show the prompt

Read the prompt once, then give students two minutes to reread it and think about it.

> ### The Surprise Outside
>
> You are at home studying for an important test when your friend calls and says, "You're not going to believe what I found in front of my place!" You run out the door and rush over to your friend's home.
>
> - Write a story about what happens next.
> - Be sure to include details in your response.

Step 2: Discuss the prompt

Have a class discussion about who and what students see in their mental images of the scenario. Ask questions to help the brainstorming:

- What might the friend have found?
- What discovery would make you want to call your friend right away?
- How can the second friend get to the first friend's house?
- What test are they studying for?
- Where outside of the house might the surprise be? Would it be on a porch, on a step, in the front yard?
- What happens when the friends get together?

Step 3: Enact the prompt

Here are suggestions for how students could approach the enactment.

1. Have one student act as the person who discovers something amazing at his or her home and another as the friend who has been studying when the phone rings. Enact the phone call with the friend responding by throwing his or her books on the floor and running out the door. Use a telephone as an optional prompt.

2. To extend the scene, have students enact the first friend's discovery of the item at the beginning as well as what the two friends decide to do after they meet.

3. Consider making the unbelievable discovery lead to a moral dilemma. For example, the discovery could be an answer key to the test they are studying for. The actors then decide whether to memorize the answer sheet for the next day's test.

Step 4: Discuss the enactment

Consider the following discussion questions.

- What are the characters' names? How old are they?
- How long have the two been friends?
- What is the setting (time and location) of the scene?
- Was the second friend just as excited about the discovery as the first friend? Why or why not?
- What problem or situation are the characters facing or involved in?
- What should they do next?

You may want to ask questions that help students develop specific parts of their responses, such as the hook or dialogue.

Step 5: A round of applause

Give your actors a round of applause.

Step 6: Scribe or write a prompt response

Refocus on the prompt rather than the enactment for the written response.

Step 7: Self-edit the response

Use the Standing Ovation Checklist for Speculative Prompts.

School Closed

Many times on your way to school you and your friends wish school would be closed. One day, when you arrive at the building, your wish has been granted. On the front door is a sign that says, "School Closed Until Further Notice."

- Write a story about why school is closed and what you will do until it reopens.
- Be sure to include details in your response.

Use the space below for brainstorming.

School Closed

Step 1: Show the prompt

Read the prompt once, then give students two minutes to reread it and think about it.

> ### School Closed
>
> Many times on your way to school you and your friends wish school would be closed. One day, when you arrive at the building, your wish has been granted. On the front door is a sign that says, "School Closed Until Further Notice."
>
> - Write a story about why school is closed and what you will do until it reopens.
> - Be sure to include details in your response.

Step 2: Discuss the prompt

Have a class discussion about who and what students see in their mental images of the scenario. Ask questions to help the brainstorming:

- Why might school be closed?
- Would you like it if school were closed?
- What would you do during the days with no school?

Step 3: Enact the prompt

Here are suggestions for how students could approach the enactment.

1. Have students enact what the kids do when they read the sign.
2. Have students enact what happens as the school remains closed for days and then weeks on end. Do they get bored? Do they wish to go back to school? Do they get transferred to another school?
3. Have students decide what has happened to cause the school to close and have them enact that. Would it be something that affected other buildings, too? Why didn't families get a phone call letting them know the school was closed?

Step 4: Discuss the enactment

Consider the following discussion questions.

- What are the characters' names? How old are they? How do they know each other?
- What is the setting (time and location) of the scene?
- What problem or situation are the characters facing or involved in?
- What's the name of your school?
- Have you ever wanted school to be closed? Why or why not?
- Has your school ever been unexpectedly closed? If so, why?
- What did you do on your days off?
- How does it feel to get an unexpected day off from school?
- How does it feel to get any unexpected surprise?
- How long would it take before you wanted to go back to school?

You may want to ask questions that help students develop specific parts of their responses, such as the hook or dialogue.

Step 5: A round of applause

Give your actors a round of applause.

Step 6: Scribe or write a prompt response

Refocus on the prompt rather than the enactment for the written response.

Step 7: Self-edit the response

Use the Standing Ovation Checklist for Speculative Prompts.

A Friend in Need

A good friend is feeling very sad and won't tell you why. The friend is getting grumpier every day.

- Write about what could be making your friend unhappy and what you could do to make him or her feel better.
- Be sure to include details in your response.

Use the space below for brainstorming.

A Friend in Need

Step 1: Show the prompt

Read the prompt once, then give students two minutes to reread it and think about it.

> ### A Friend in Need
>
> A good friend is feeling very sad and won't tell you why. The friend is getting grumpier every day.
>
> - Write about what could be making your friend unhappy and what you could do to make him or her feel better.
> - Be sure to include details in your response.

Step 2: Discuss the prompt

Have a class discussion about who and what students see in their mental images of the scenario. Ask questions to help the brainstorming:

- What kinds of things could the friend be grumpy about?
- What are some small things and big things that could make someone unhappy?
- How do you look when you are grumpy?
- How could you get the friend to tell you what is bothering him or her?
- What can you do after you find out what's bothering your friend?

Step 3: Enact the prompt

Here are suggestions for how students could approach the enactment.

1. Have students pretend to be at different places in the school during the school day such as in line for lunch, outside for gym or recess, or walking to and from school. One student plays the role of the grumpy child and one or more others play the friend(s) coaxing the sad student to talk about what's wrong.

2. To extend the scene, have the student reveal what is making her or him sad and have the other students react to that. Perhaps they try to cheer up their friend. How would they do that?

Step 4: Discuss the enactment

Consider the following discussion questions.

- What are the characters' names? How old are they? How do they know each other?
- What is the setting (time and location) of the scene?
- What problem or situation are the characters facing or involved in?
- Why was the child grumpy?
- How would you feel if the same thing happened to you?
- How did the other kids feel when they found out what was bothering their friend?
- Why did the friend finally reveal the reason for being grumpy?
- What have you done or can you do to cheer up a friend?
- What have your friends done to cheer you up?
- Are you a good friend? Why or why not?

You may want to ask questions that help students develop specific parts of their responses, such as the hook or dialogue.

Step 5: A round of applause

Give your actors a round of applause.

Step 6: Scribe or write a prompt response

Refocus on the prompt rather than the enactment for the written response.

Step 7: Self-edit the response

Use the Standing Ovation Checklist for Speculative Prompts.

Me? A Winner?

Your principal just called you to his office to tell you that you are going to receive a surprise award. The award will be presented at a school-wide assembly program this afternoon.

- Write about the award you were chosen to receive, what it was given for, and how you felt receiving it.
- Be sure to include details in your response.

Use the space below for brainstorming.

Me? A Winner?

Step 1: Show the prompt

Read the prompt once, then give students two minutes to reread it and think about it.

Me? A Winner?

Your principal just called you to his office to tell you that you are going to receive a surprise award. The award will be presented at a school-wide assembly program this afternoon.

- Write about the award you were chosen to receive, what it was given for, and how you felt receiving it.
- Be sure to include details in your response.

Step 2: Discuss the prompt

Have a class discussion about who and what students see in their mental images of the scenario. Ask questions to help the brainstorming:

- What could the award be for?
- What kind of award would a principal give to a student?
- What would the award look like?
- Could it be a group award instead of an individual award?
- Why do you think you were chosen? What are you good at?

Step 3: Enact the prompt

Here are suggestions for how students could approach the enactment.

1. Have one student act as the principal and another student as the award recipient. You could also add a teacher and a few classmates. Begin with the principal calling the student to the office over the phone or PA system. Have the student react upon hearing the news and walk nervously to the principal's office. The principal invites the student into his office and they both are seated. Then the principal tells the student why he or she has been summoned.

2. Maybe there was a mistake, and the student doesn't deserve the award. Enact the moral dilemma she or he faces in telling the principal that someone else really should get the award.

3. Have students enact a group award, such as a class award for writing or a team award.

Step 4: Discuss the enactment

Consider the following discussion questions.

- What are the characters' names? How old are they? How do they know each other?
- What is the setting (time and location) of the scene?
- What problem or situation are the characters facing or involved in?
- How did the student feel about getting the award?
- Have you ever received an award in school? For what?
- How did you feel? How did your friends feel about you receiving it?
- Was it an individual award or a class award?
- What prize did you receive (trophy, medal, money, etc.)?
- Is there a downside to winning an award? If so, what is it?
- Would you rather receive an award as a surprise or would you like to know ahead of time?
- How would it (or did it) feel to make an acceptance speech?
- What award could you give to your principal?

You may want to ask questions that help students develop specific parts of their responses, such as the hook or dialogue.

Step 5: A round of applause

Give your actors a round of applause.

Step 6: Scribe or write a prompt response

Refocus on the prompt rather than the enactment for the written response.

Step 7: Self-edit the response

Use the Standing Ovation Checklist for Speculative Prompts.

The Class Pet

It's your turn to bring home the class pet for the weekend. You have everything you need in your backpack. The moment your mother sees you coming through the front door, her mouth falls open and she gasps.

- Write a story about what type of pet it is and what you would do to take care of it over the weekend.
- Be sure to include details in your response.

Use the space below for brainstorming.

The Class Pet

Step 1: Show the prompt

Read the prompt once, then give students two minutes to reread it and think about it.

> ### The Class Pet
>
> It's your turn to bring home the class pet for the weekend. You have everything you need in your backpack. The moment your mother sees you coming through the front door, her mouth falls open and she gasps.
>
> - Write a story about what type of pet it is and what you would do to take care of it over the weekend.
> - Be sure to include details in your response.

Step 2: Discuss the prompt

Have a class discussion about who and what students see in their mental images of the scenario. Ask questions to help the brainstorming:

- What kind of pet could it be?
- Why is the mom so surprised?
- What is it like to take care of a pet? Is the pet in this story going to be different? How?

Step 3: Enact the prompt

Here are suggestions for how students could approach the enactment.

1. Have one student play the role of the mother and one play the role of the student, with a stuffed animal or other prop as the pet. Enact the scene where the student walks in with the pet and the mother reacts with surprise. Why is she so surprised? What will happen next?
2. Enact the same scene, but have one student play the role of the pet. He or she could act silly or disruptive. For example, if the pet is a rabbit, it could be jumping a lot and knocking things over.
3. Have students enact the scenes from both characters' perspectives immediately before this meeting. Does the student know his mother will be surprised? Does the pet act silly or disruptive? Did the mother have plans for the weekend?

Step 4: Discuss the enactment

Consider the following discussion questions.

- What are the characters' names? How old are they?
- What is the setting (time and location) of the scene?
- What problem or situation are the characters facing or involved in?
- How did the mother feel?
- How did the student feel?
- Do you or have you ever had a pet at home?
- Were you responsible for taking care of the pet? Why or why not?
- What's involved with the care of a pet?
- What type of pet would be a good class pet? Why?
- Who would take care of a class pet, and when?
- What would you name the class pet?
- Would you volunteer to take the pet home and care for it over the weekend?
- What would your family's reaction be if you came home with the class rabbit or other pet?
- If your parent was upset about the pet, what could you do to help her or him feel better?
- Do you think the pet will make it safely through the weekend and return to school on Monday? Why or why not?

You may want to ask questions that help students develop specific parts of their responses, such as the hook or dialogue.

Step 5: A round of applause

Give your actors a round of applause.

Step 6: Scribe or write a prompt response

Refocus on the prompt rather than the enactment for the written response.

Step 7: Self-edit the response

Use the Standing Ovation Checklist for Speculative Prompts.

Selling a Cell Phone

It seems like all your friends have cell phones, and you want one, too, but your family won't allow it. They say you're not responsible enough.

Write a letter to your parent or a family adult persuading that person to let you have a cell phone. Make sure to use details to support your reasons.

Use the space below for brainstorming.

Selling a Cell Phone

Step 1: Show the prompt

Read the prompt once, then give students two minutes to reread it and think about it.

Selling a Cell Phone

It seems like all your friends have cell phones, and you want one, too, but your family won't allow it. They say you're not responsible enough.

Write a letter to your parent or a family adult persuading that person to let you have a cell phone. Make sure to use details to support your reasons.

Step 2: Discuss the prompt

Have a class discussion about who and what students see in their mental images of the scenario. Help them think about the stance they will take on the issue and reasons they might use to support that stance. They should also think about alternate points of view and prepare to use facts and details that persuade the reader to understand and accept their point of view. Ask questions to help the brainstorming:

- Why do you want a cell phone?
- Why might your family not want you to have one?
- What are some reasons for having a cell phone that your family might agree with?

Step 3: Enact the prompt

Here are suggestions for how students could approach the enactment.

1. Have one student play the role of the child who wants a cell phone and one or two students play the role of the adults. Enact a scene in which the student is arguing for a cell phone and the adult(s) is saying no. Make sure both sides provide reasons.

2. For an alternative point of view on the subject, have your students enact a scene in which the adult wants the child to have a cell phone—perhaps to make it easier to keep in touch—but the student doesn't want one. Is it harder to come up with reasons for both roles when their positions are reversed? This can help students identify strong arguments as well as alternate points of view.

Step 4: Discuss the enactment

Consider the following discussion questions.

- Was the child in the enactment persuasive?
- Who had a stronger argument in the enactment, the adult or the student?
- How did the adult feel?
- How did the student feel?
- What compromise might be reached on this issue?
- Think of a time when you tried to change your parent's mind. Were you successful? Why or why not?
- What do you do after your parents say no to something you want?
- Do you have a cell phone? If not, do you want one? Why or why not?
- Do many of your friends have cell phones?
- How could you show your family that you are responsible enough to have a cell phone?
- What are the positive aspects of having a cell phone? What are the negative aspects?

You may want to ask questions that help students develop specific parts of their responses, such as the hook, supporting reasons, and details.

Step 5: A round of applause

Give your actors a round of applause.

Step 6: Scribe or write a prompt response

Refocus on the prompt rather than the enactment for the written response.

Step 7: Self-edit the response

Use the Standing Ovation Checklist for Persuasive Prompts.

Message in a Bottle

You find yourself shipwrecked on a deserted island. Lucky for you, the island was once a popular tourist spot and still has luxurious hotels with electricity, a working amusement park, beautiful beaches, restaurants, and food stores with stocked refrigerators. After searching the island, however, you realize you are totally alone, without telephones or computers.

Write a letter to place in a bottle and toss in the ocean in hopes of it reaching somebody who will contact your family and friends. In your letter, try to persuade your family and friends to rescue you and bring you home forever or move to the island and live with you there forever. Support your position with reasons and details.

Use the space below for brainstorming.

Message in a Bottle

Prompt type: Persuasive

Step 1: Show the prompt

Read the prompt once, then give students two minutes to reread it and think about it.

> **Message in a Bottle**
>
> You find yourself shipwrecked on a deserted island. Lucky for you, the island was once a popular tourist spot and still has luxurious hotels with electricity, a working amusement park, beautiful beaches, restaurants, and food stores with stocked refrigerators. After searching the island, however, you realize you are totally alone, without telephones or computers.
>
> Write a letter to place in a bottle and toss in the ocean in hopes of it reaching somebody who will contact your family and friends. In your letter, try to persuade your family and friends to rescue you and bring you home forever or move to the island and live with you there forever. Support your position with reasons and details.

Step 2: Discuss the prompt

Have a class discussion about who and what students see in their mental images of the scenario. Help them think about the stance they will take on the issue and reasons they might use to support that stance. They should also think about alternate points of view and prepare to use facts and details that persuade the reader to understand and accept their point of view. Ask questions to help the brainstorming:

- Have you ever been on an island?
- Would you like being on an island?
- Do you like being alone? How does it feel?
- Who would you miss if you were alone on an island? Why?
- Would you be concerned for your safety on the island?
- Would you like your family and friends to join you on your island? Why or why not?
- Would you leave if you could?

Step 3: Enact the prompt

Here are suggestions for how students could approach the enactment.

1. Have one student enact being shipwrecked, exploring the island, writing the note, rolling it up, stuffing it in a bottle, and tossing it into the sea. The student could narrate the note as he or she writes it, so the audience can hear what is on it. Have other students play the roles of different props, such as water (for example, by holding up blue paper or a blue bed sheet and making it roll like waves), trees, and animals.

2. Have students enact the water: on one side of the water a child plays the role of the person shipwrecked on the island and on the other side students portray the family and friends at home. What are the family and friends doing while the child is lost on the island?

3. Have the family and/or friends find the bottle, take out the note, and read it. After a jubilant outburst, the family and/or friends discuss the contents of the letter and decide what to do next.

Step 4: Discuss the enactment

Consider the following discussion questions.

- Do you think the family and friends would prefer to move to the island, or would they rather have their child return home? Why?
- If you were shipwrecked, would you prefer to stay on the island or come home again? Why?
- What do you think your family would choose? Why?
- What do you think happened to make the island deserted?
- How would life be different on the island once your family came?
- How would life be different for you if you returned home?
- How would you have changed as a person from this experience?

You may want to ask questions that help students develop specific parts of their responses, such as the hook, supporting reasons, and details.

Step 5: A round of applause

Give your actors a round of applause.

Step 6: Scribe or write a prompt response

Refocus on the prompt rather than the enactment for the written response.

Step 7: Self-edit the response

Use the Standing Ovation Checklist for Persuasive Prompts.

Energy Saving Schedule

In order to save energy, the school board is thinking about putting all schools in your district on a four-day school week. If this happens, each school day will be ninety minutes longer than it is now.

Write a letter to your school board arguing for or against the idea. Make sure to support your stance with reasons and details.

Use the space below for brainstorming.

Energy Saving Schedule

Step 1: Show the prompt

Read the prompt once, then give students two minutes to reread it and think about it.

> ### Energy Saving Schedule
>
> In order to save energy, the school board is thinking about putting all schools in your district on a four-day school week. If this happens, each school day will be ninety minutes longer than it is now.
>
> Write a letter to your school board arguing for or against the idea. Make sure to support your stance with reasons and details.

Step 2: Discuss the prompt

Have a class discussion about who and what students see in their mental images of the scenario. Help them think about the stance they will take on the issue and reasons they might use to support that stance. They should also think about alternate points of view and prepare to use facts and details that persuade the reader to understand and accept their point of view. Ask questions to help the brainstorming:

- How would closing school one full day per week help save energy?
- How could you calculate how much money would be saved by this idea?
- Would this schedule interfere with things you normally do after school?
- How would this schedule impact the schedules of extracurricular activities such as band, athletics, clubs, and chorus?
- How would the schedule affect how you get home from school?

Step 3: Enact the prompt

Here are suggestions for how students could approach the enactment.

1. Have one group of students enact what happens when a typical school day ends but now the students still have ninety minutes more in class. How do the students feel? Perhaps they are falling asleep at their desks, rubbing their hungry stomachs, doodling due to difficulty concentrating, or gazing out the window at rush hour traffic. Have a student play the role of the teacher, too.

2. Have students enact various activities that could be done on the extra day off from school. Activities might include sleeping late, watching TV, texting friends, going to the library, doing chores at home, baby-sitting or taking care of siblings, and more. Also, since every weekend is a three-day weekend, perhaps students can participate in more organized activities such as sports teams or take more frequent family vacations.

Step 4: Discuss the enactment

Consider the following discussion questions.

- How did the students feel during the extra ninety minutes of school per day?
- How did they feel during the extra days off?
- What would you do on this extra day each week?
- Which schedule would you prefer, the four-day or five-day week?
- Can you think of a better way to save energy in your school?
- How would this schedule impact your family? How would they feel about this idea?
- How could you make the extra ninety minutes easier to handle?
- How do you think your teachers would feel about the schedule?

You may want to ask questions that help students develop specific parts of their responses, such as the hook, supporting reasons, and details.

Step 5: A round of applause

Give your actors a round of applause.

Step 6: Scribe or write a prompt response

Refocus on the prompt rather than the enactment for the written response.

Step 7: Self-edit the response

Use the Standing Ovation Checklist for Persuasive Prompts.

School Improvement Is Up to You

People are always looking for ways to improve schools, and some of the best ideas come from students. Your principal is giving students the opportunity to submit ideas for ways to improve your school. Think of ONE change you would like to see happen at your school to make it better. Write a letter to your principal that would convince her or him to accept your idea. Be sure to support your idea with detailed reasons why it would improve the school.

Use the space below for brainstorming.

School Improvement Is Up to You

Step 1: Show the prompt

Read the prompt once, then give students two minutes to reread it and think about it.

> ### School Improvement Is Up to You
>
> People are always looking for ways to improve schools, and some of the best ideas come from students. Your principal is giving students the opportunity to submit ideas for ways to improve your school. Think of ONE change you would like to see happen at your school to make it better. Write a letter to your principal that would convince her or him to accept your idea. Be sure to support your idea with detailed reasons why it would improve the school.

Step 2: Discuss the prompt

Have a class discussion about who and what students see in their mental images of the scenario. Help them think about the stance they will take on the issue and reasons they might use to support that stance. They should also think about alternate points of view and prepare to use facts and details that persuade the reader to understand and accept their point of view. Ask questions to help the brainstorming:

- What are some things you would like to change in your school? What one change do you think is most important?
- Why would you like to make this change?
- How will this change impact students? How will it impact teachers and staff? How about parents?
- What are some reasons not to do your change?
- How do you think your principal will react to your idea?
- How will your classmates react to your idea?

Step 3: Enact the prompt

Here are suggestions for how students could approach the enactment.

1. Have the enactment team come up with a change and enact what would happen if it is made. For example, if the suggestion is to add fifteen minutes to lunch period each day, students could enact possible activities done during the extra time. Encourage them to enact any possible downsides to their improvement, too. You might have several individuals or enactment teams give performances showing their ideas.

2. As an extension of idea #1, have students enact the problem their idea would solve before they enact the solution.

3. Have students enact the roles of many school figures, including students, teachers, the principal, and other staff. How does the change affect each of these people?

4. Have students enact a brainstorming meeting involving all these players. During the meeting, different students present ideas for improvement along with reasons why they are important. The principal asks questions in order to help make a decision (such as how much will it cost? What problem will it fix? How will it affect students? What problems might arise because of it?).

Step 4: Discuss the enactment

Consider the following discussion questions.

- Which idea do you think was the best? Why?
- Do you think students would have better improvement ideas than adults? Why?
- If your principal is going to choose only one improvement idea, what do you think would be the fairest way for her or him to choose?
- Do you think it would be hard to choose one improvement? Why?
- How would you feel if your improvement was selected?

You may want to ask questions that help students develop specific parts of their responses, such as the hook, supporting reasons, and details.

Step 5: A round of applause

Give your actors a round of applause.

Step 6: Scribe or write a prompt response

Refocus on the prompt rather than the enactment for the written response.

Step 7: Self-edit the response

Use the Standing Ovation Checklist for Persuasive Prompts.

Concerned About Curfews

Lawmakers and families often impose curfews on kids and teens, making it against the law or family rules to be out later than a certain time. Are you in favor of curfews or against them? Choose a side and write a letter to your mayor or parent arguing for your point of view. Be sure to support your argument with detailed reasons.

Use the space below for brainstorming.

Concerned About Curfews

Prompt type: Persuasive

Step 1: Show the prompt

Read the prompt once, then give students two minutes to reread it and think about it.

> ### Concerned About Curfews
>
> Lawmakers and families often impose curfews on kids and teens, making it against the law or family rules to be out later than a certain time. Are you in favor of curfews or against them? Choose a side and write a letter to your mayor or parent arguing for your point of view. Be sure to support your argument with detailed reasons.

Step 2: Discuss the prompt

Have a class discussion about who and what students see in their mental images of the scenario. Help them think about the stance they will take on the issue and reasons they might use to support that stance. They should also think about alternate points of view and prepare to use facts and details that persuade the reader to understand and accept their point of view. Ask questions to help the brainstorming:

- What is the goal of a curfew?
- Do curfews achieve their goal? How do you know?
- What happens if a kid or teen breaks a curfew? What are the consequences? What do you think the consequences should be?
- Do your parents give you a curfew at home? If so, what happens if you break your curfew? Has this ever happened to you?
- What are some reasons kids, teens, or adults might be opposed to curfews?

Step 3: Enact the prompt

Here are suggestions for how students could approach the enactment.

1. Darken the classroom by turning off the lights to simulate night time. Have students enact a scene in which a kid or teen has missed curfew and arrives home ten minutes late. Students play the roles of the child and one or two adults. The kid rushes to get home and finds his or her family standing in the doorway, almost blocking the entrance. They are worried and visibly upset. Have each participant explain his or her side of the situation. The kid explains why he or she was late and the family explains why they are upset.

2. Enact a kid or teen's point of view with a scene in which kids are doing something fun or exciting— or perhaps doing something to help others, such as a community service project. As curfew draws near, they have to stop what they're doing to go home.

3. Enact the family's point of view with a scene in which they are worrying about their child or trying to find him or her.

Step 4: Discuss the enactment

Consider the following discussion questions.

- Who was more effective in persuading the audience during the enactment, the family or the kid?
- How does it feel to have a curfew?
- How did the parent(s) feel in this scene?
- Is there ever a good reason for breaking a curfew?
- Does gender affect curfew decisions? How?
- How does age affect curfew decisions?
- Should there ever be a curfew for parents?
- If you disagree with a rule, do you still obey it? Why or why not?
- How do you think being late for a curfew affects a family's relationships?

You may want to ask questions that help students develop specific parts of their responses, such as the hook, supporting reasons, and details.

Step 5: A round of applause

Give your actors a round of applause.

Step 6: Scribe or write a prompt response

Refocus on the prompt rather than the enactment for the written response.

Step 7: Self-edit the response

Use the Standing Ovation Checklist for Persuasive Prompts.

Being Part of a Family

Danitra's Family Reunion
by Nikki Grimes

On the Fourth of July,
my cousins and I
ran sack races,
played kickball
and tug-of-war
before
we heard
our stomachs
growl.
We stopped for
deviled eggs,
buttered corn,
coleslaw,
fried chicken,
potato salad, and
Strawberry Pie Jubilee.
We sipped lemonade
and listened to
Grandma Brown's stories
of when our folks were little.
Then Uncle Joe
handed out prizes
for this year's graduates
and for the best all-round student,
which I won.
By the time
the day was done,
I was full of fun
and food
and warm feelings,
knowing that I am more
than just me.
I am part
of a family.

Writing Assignment

Have you ever spent a whole day with your extended family? Have you spent a whole day with a friend's family? Write about an experience that helped you understand the value of family. A family does not have to be the traditional mom and dad and siblings. Families may be made up of friends and their families or even the students in your class. Include the following in your response:

- What event made you realize you are part of a family? When did you realize this?
- How do you feel about being part of this group?
- What are the positive and negative aspects of families?
- Be sure to include details, reasons, and examples in your response.

From *See It, Be It, Write It: Using Performing Arts to Improve Writing Skills and Test Scores* by Hope Sara Blecher-Sass, Ed.D., & Maryellen Moffitt, copyright © 2010. Free Spirit Publishing Inc., Minneapolis, MN; 800-735-7323; www.freespirit.com. This page may be reproduced for individual, classroom, and small group work only. For other uses, contact www.freespirit.com/company/permissions.cfm.

Being Part of a Family

Step 1: Show the prompt

Read the prompt once, including the writing task at the end of the poem, then give students two minutes to reread it and think about it.

> **Being Part of a Family**
>
> **Danitra's Family Reunion**
> by Nikki Grimes
>
> On the Fourth of July,
> my cousins and I
> ran sack races,
> played kickball
> and tug-of-war
> before
> we heard
> our stomachs
> growl.
> We stopped for
> deviled eggs,
> buttered corn,
> coleslaw,
> fried chicken,
> potato salad, and
> Strawberry Pie Jubilee.
> We sipped lemonade
> and listened to
> Grandma Brown's stories
> of when our folks were little.
> Then Uncle Joe
> handed out prizes
> for this year's graduates
> and for the best all-round student,
> which I won.
> By the time
> the day was done,
> I was full of fun
> and food
> and warm feelings,
> knowing that I am more
> than just me.
> I am part
> of a family.
>
> **Writing Assignment**
> Have you ever spent a whole day with your extended family? Have you spent a whole day with a friend's family? Write about an experience that helped you understand the value of family. A family does not have to be the traditional mom and dad and siblings. Families may be made up of friends and their families or even the students in your class. Include the following in your response:
>
> - What event made you realize you are part of a family? When did you realize this?
> - How do you feel about being part of this group?
> - What are the positive and negative aspects of families?
> - Be sure to include details, reasons, and examples in your response.

Step 2: Discuss the prompt

Have a class discussion about who and what students see in their mental images of the poem and how they might answer the writing task questions. Help them think about personal connections they can make to the poem, including text-to-self, text-to-text, or text-to-world connections. Ask questions to help the brainstorming:

- What is the title of the poem? Why do you think it is called that?
- Who is the author of the poem?
- Are you familiar with other poems or books by Nikki Grimes?
- Who are the people in the poem?
- How do they know each other?
- What is the setting (time and location) of the poem?
- What realization does Danitra have at the end of the poem?
- Have you ever been to a big family event or a family reunion? What was it like? What did you do?

Step 3: Enact the prompt

Here are suggestions for how students could approach the enactment.

1. Have students play the roles of Grandma Brown, Uncle Joe, Danitra, and the cousins, and enact the various scenes in the poem. Kids can pretend to have a tug-of-war, to eat, and to sip lemonade. They can gather around Grandma and listen to her tell a story about one of the cousin's parents, and Uncle Joe can give out prizes.

2. To extend suggestion #1, have all the actors gather to shake hands with each other or to make a circle with their arms on each other's shoulders to show unity as a big family.

3. Enact the car rides to and from the reunion for Danitra and her immediate family. How does Danitra's perspective about her larger family change between the two rides?

Step 4: Discuss the enactment

Consider the following discussion questions.

- Did the kids have fun playing games? What game looked like the most fun? Why?
- Have you ever tasted the foods mentioned in the poem? Which one do you like and why?
- What is your favorite food to eat when you have a family event?
- What story did Grandma Brown tell? Why did she tell it?
- What did the prize look like that Uncle Joe handed out? Was it a trophy, a medal, or something else?
- What has made you realize you are part of a family?
- How does it feel to be a part of a family?

You may want to ask questions that help students develop specific parts of their responses, such as the hook and the personal connection.

Step 5: A round of applause

Give your actors a round of applause.

Step 6: Scribe or write a prompt response

Refocus on the prompt rather than the enactment for the written response.

Step 7: Self-edit the response

Use the Standing Ovation Checklist for Poetry Prompts.

Cool Things You Learn in School

My Excellent Education
by Kenn Nesbitt

How to juggle.
How to hop.
How to make
my knuckles pop.

How to whinny.
How to cluck.
How to talk
like Donald Duck.

How to wiggle
both my ears.
How to fake
convincing tears.

How to yo-yo.
Capture flies.
Roll my tongue
and cross my eyes.

How to make a
piggy snout.
How to make
my eyes bug out.

That's a list
of all the cool
stuff I learned
to do in school.

Writing Assignment
Think of something cool that you learned in school. It may be something your teacher never intended to teach you. Write a composition about the cool thing you learned. Include the following:

- What was the cool thing you learned in school?
- Why was it cool to learn?
- If you could teach that thing to someone else, who would you teach it to and why?
- Be sure to include details, reasons, and examples in your response.

From *See It, Be It, Write It: Using Performing Arts to Improve Writing Skills and Test Scores* by Hope Sara Blecher-Sass, Ed.D., & Maryellen Moffitt, copyright © 2010. Free Spirit Publishing Inc., Minneapolis, MN; 800-735-7323; www.freespirit.com. This page may be reproduced for individual, classroom, and small group work only. For other uses, contact www.freespirit.com/company/permissions.cfm.

Cool Things You Learn in School

Step 1: Show the prompt

Read the prompt once, including the writing task at the end of the poem, then give students two minutes to reread it and think about it.

> ### Cool Things You Learn in School
>
> **My Excellent Education**
> by Kenn Nesbitt
>
> How to juggle.
> How to hop.
> How to make
> my knuckles pop.
>
> How to whinny.
> How to cluck.
> How to talk
> like Donald Duck.
>
> How to wiggle
> both my ears.
> How to fake
> convincing tears.
>
> How to yo-yo.
> Capture flies.
> Roll my tongue
> and cross my eyes.
>
> How to make a
> piggy snout.
> How to make
> my eyes bug out.
>
> That's a list
> of all the cool
> stuff I learned
> to do in school.
>
> **Writing Assignment**
> Think of something cool that you learned in school. It may be something your teacher never intended to teach you. Write a composition about the cool thing you learned. Include the following:
>
> - What was the cool thing you learned in school?
> - Why was it cool to learn?
> - If you could teach that thing to someone else, who would you teach it to and why?
> - Be sure to include details, reasons, and examples in your response.

Step 2: Discuss the prompt

Have a class discussion about who and what students see in their mental images of the poem and how they might answer the writing task questions. Help them think about personal connections they can make to the poem, including text-to-self, text-to-text, or text-to-world connections. Ask questions to help the brainstorming:

- What is the title of the poem?
- Who is the author of the poem?
- Are you familiar with other poems written by Kenn Nesbitt?
- What is happening in this poem?
- What is the setting (time and location) of the poem?
- Does the title fit the poem? Why or why not?
- What unexpected thing have you learned in school? What have you learned other than what your teachers might have wanted you to learn?
- What fun story can you tell about any of your years in school?

Step 3: Enact the prompt

Here are suggestions for how students could approach the enactment.

1. Have students enact all the activities described in the poem, from juggling to making their eyes pop.
2. To follow up, have students enact some of the things they have learned in their school that were not academic. This can be social (how to make friends) and useful (using a locker).

Step 4: Discuss the enactment

Consider the following discussion questions.

- What looked like the most important thing learned in school?
- What looked like the most fun?
- Why do students go to school?
- What is the most important thing you learned in school that did not come from a book? What was the most important thing you learned that did not come from your teacher?
- What memory of school do you think you will remember the longest? Why?
- What is the most fun you ever had at school? Why was it so much fun?

You may want to ask questions that help students develop specific parts of their responses, such as the hook and the personal connection.

Step 5: A round of applause

Give your actors a round of applause.

Step 6: Scribe or write a prompt response

Refocus on the prompt rather than the enactment for the written response.

Step 7: Self-edit the response

Use the Standing Ovation Checklist for Poetry Prompts.

A Birthday Superpower Surprise

The Not So Super Superpower
by Tammy Scott

Yesterday was my birthday. I'd planned a year;
To wish for a power, but I was unclear.

Running real fast or flying high in the sky;
Were some of the powers I wanted to try.

Reading other kids' minds while sitting in school;
Now that is a power that would have been cool.

Disappearing or turning things into ice;
A few of the powers that would have been nice.

But today I got an unhappy surprise.
I realized it just as I opened my eyes.

Could this be happening? It's not what I chose!
The superpower seems to be with my nose.

Every scent that wafts through the room I can smell.
Already, I sense that this year won't go well.

Good smells and bad ones drifting in through
    my snout.
Not at all what my power should be about!

Perhaps, in time, I'll find a use for this skill.
But right now I don't think that I ever will.

I'll just need to learn to live without smelling.
For how long this will last, there is no telling.

At least now it's clear how my wishing must be.
On my birthday next year, I'll wish to be me.

Writing Assignment

Have you ever wished to change something about yourself? What did you wish for? Why? Write a composition about what you wished for. Include the following:

- What did you wish for and why did you wish for it?
- If you got what you wished for, explain how and why. Was the change as good as you hoped it would be? Why or why not?
- If you didn't get what you wished for, tell why not. How did it feel not to get it? Do you still wish for the same thing? Why or why not?
- Be sure to include details in your response.

From *See It, Be It, Write It: Using Performing Arts to Improve Writing Skills and Test Scores* by Hope Sara Blecher-Sass, Ed.D., & Maryellen Moffitt, copyright © 2010. Free Spirit Publishing Inc., Minneapolis, MN; 800-735-7323; www.freespirit.com. This page may be reproduced for individual, classroom, and small group work only. For other uses, contact www.freespirit.com/company/permissions.cfm.

A Birthday Superpower Surprise

Step 1: Show the prompt

Read the prompt once, including the writing task at the end of the poem, then give students two minutes to reread it and think about it.

> ### A Birthday Superpower Surprise
>
> **The Not So Super Superpower**
> by Tammy Scott
>
> Yesterday was my birthday. I'd planned a year;
> To wish for a power, but I was unclear.
>
> Running real fast or flying high in the sky;
> Were some of the powers I wanted to try.
>
> Reading other kids' minds while sitting in school;
> Now that is a power that would have been cool.
>
> Disappearing or turning things into ice;
> A few of the powers that would have been nice.
>
> But today I got an unhappy surprise.
> I realized it just as I opened my eyes.
>
> Could this be happening? It's not what I chose!
> The superpower seems to be with my nose.
>
> Every scent that wafts through the room I can smell.
> Already, I sense that this year won't go well.
>
> Good smells and bad ones drifting in through my snout.
> Not at all what my power should be about!
>
> Perhaps, in time, I'll find a use for this skill.
> But right now I don't think that I ever will.
>
> I'll just need to learn to live without smelling.
> For how long this will last, there is no telling.
>
> At least now it's clear how my wishing must be.
> On my birthday next year, I'll wish to be me.
>
> **Writing Assignment**
> Have you ever wished to change something about yourself? What did you wish for? Why? Write a composition about what you wished for. Include the following:
>
> - What did you wish for and why did you wish for it?
> - If you got what you wished for, explain how and why. Was the change as good as you hoped it would be? Why or why not?
> - If you didn't get what you wished for, tell why not. How did it feel not to get it? Do you still wish for the same thing? Why or why not?
> - Be sure to include details in your response.

Step 2: Discuss the prompt

Have a class discussion about who and what students see in their mental images of the poem and how they might answer the writing task questions. Help them think about personal connections they can make to the poem, including text-to-self, text-to-text, or text-to-world connections. Ask questions to help the brainstorming:

- What is the title of the poem?
- How does the title relate to the poem?
- Who is the character in the poem?
- What is the character doing?
- Why is the superpower not such a good birthday surprise?
- What is the setting (time and location) for the events in the poem?
- What type of superpower would you wish for and why?
- What if your birthday surprise were to be granted the opposite of the superpower you wished for? What would you do? How would you feel?

Step 3: Enact the prompt

Here are suggestions for how students could approach the enactment.

1. Have students enact the excitement they feel in the days before a birthday. The actors could discuss what they are wishing for, what they may have received as past gifts, or what they think they will actually get. The enactment may then shift to the day when the student in the poem realized he was given the gift of a super sense of smell. The students act out what it was that made them realize that they had this new power, and then what their first day was like with this heightened sense of smell.

2. Another option is to have the enactment group decide on one or several other superpowers to receive as a birthday gift and enact what happens next. Are there negative as well as positive effects of these superpowers?

Step 4: Discuss the enactment

Consider the following discussion questions.

- Did the person like the superpower? How do you know?
- Was it what he or she expected?
- What were the positive and negative aspects of having super smelling power?
- Did you ever wish for something and get the exact opposite?
- How did you feel?
- If you could have any one wish, what would it be?
- If you could have any one wish for your best friend, what would it be?

You may want to ask questions that help students develop specific parts of their responses, such as the hook and the personal connection.

Step 5: A round of applause

Give your actors a round of applause.

Step 6: Scribe or write a prompt response

Refocus on the prompt rather than the enactment for the written response.

Step 7: Self-edit the response

Use the Standing Ovation Checklist for Poetry Prompts.

A Favorite Memory

Snowy Hopes
by John DeLaurentis

Early in the morning,
Snow cuddled up to the glass
of my window pane.
I pulled myself from bed
and dressed very fast
with thoughts in my brain.

Will school open today?
Or will the snow piled high
cause it to close?
I crept to my parents' room
And my mother said "Hi.
School's closed, I suppose."

My snowy hopes to play
Outside in the winter chill
Came true at last.
The radio said, "School's closed."
My insides felt a thrill
As I ran outside fast.

The whole morning I built
the biggest, wettest, snowman
with my good friend Bill.
We laughed and talked
and across the yard ran,
Until our bodies felt the chill.

At lunch, my mom fed me
Hot chocolate and fries
That warmed me like a fire.
I smiled with delight
At warm apple pie,
I had all I could desire.

Writing Assignment

The child in this poem describes a happy memory of a day spent playing and eating favorite foods. Think of a time you spent a whole day doing things you loved. Write a composition about what you did. Include the following:

- Who did you spend your day with?
- What activities did you do?

From *See It, Be It, Write It: Using Performing Arts to Improve Writing Skills and Test Scores* by Hope Sara Blecher-Sass, Ed.D., & Maryellen Moffitt, copyright © 2010. Free Spirit Publishing Inc., Minneapolis, MN; 800-735-7323; www.freespirit.com. This page may be reproduced for individual, classroom, and small group work only. For other uses, contact www.freespirit.com/company/permissions.cfm.

A Favorite Memory

Step 1: Show the prompt

Read the prompt once, including the writing task at the end of the poem, then give students two minutes to reread it and think about it.

A Favorite Memory

Snowy Hopes
by John DeLaurentis

Early in the morning,
Snow cuddled up to the glass
of my window pane.
I pulled myself from bed
and dressed very fast
with thoughts in my brain.

Will school open today?
Or will the snow piled high
cause it to close?
I crept to my parents' room
And my mother said "Hi.
School's closed, I suppose."

My snowy hopes to play
Outside in the winter chill
Came true at last.
The radio said, "School's closed."
My insides felt a thrill
As I ran outside fast.

The whole morning I built
the biggest, wettest, snowman
with my good friend Bill.
We laughed and talked
and across the yard ran,
Until our bodies felt the chill.

At lunch, my mom fed me
Hot chocolate and fries
That warmed me like a fire.
I smiled with delight
At warm apple pie,
I had all I could desire.

Writing Assignment
The child in this poem describes a happy memory of a day spent playing and eating favorite foods. Think of a time you spent a whole day doing things you loved. Write a composition about what you did. Include the following:

- Who did you spend your day with?
- What activities did you do?

Step 2: Discuss the prompt

Have a class discussion about who and what students see in their mental images of the poem and how they might answer the writing task questions. Help them think about personal connections they can make to the poem, including text-to-self, text-to-text, or text-to-world connections. Ask questions to help the brainstorming:

- What is the title of the poem? Why do you think it is called that?
- Who is the author of the poem?
- What is happening in this poem?
- What is the setting of this poem?
- Who are the people in the poem?
- Have you ever awoke to see a deep blanket of snow outside? How did you feel?
- What games and activities can you do in the snow that you can't do in summer?
- Do you prefer summer or winter weather?
- Do you have friends in your neighborhood to play with?
- What was your favorite memory of a day playing in the snow? What other fun memories can you think of?
- What are some of your favorite things to do?

Step 3: Enact the prompt

Here are suggestions for how students could approach the enactment.

1. Have the students enact getting up in the morning, looking out their window, and finding a fresh covering of snow. Have a student play the role of a parent who tells the child that there is no school. How does the student react? How does the parent react?
2. Switch the setting to outdoors and ask the students to enact all the activities they do in the snow.
3. Have students enact several of their favorite activities and eating some of their favorite foods.

Step 4: Discuss the enactment

Consider the following discussion questions.

- Why do you think schools close when it snows?
- What activity looked like the most fun?
- Is there anything you don't like about snow?
- Do you enjoy certain foods or warm drinks on a cold day?
- Do you think parents like snowy days? Why or why not?
- Do you think teachers like snowy days? Why or why not?
- Do you think enjoying favorite foods or doing favorite things is even better when it comes as a surprise (like playing in the snow when you thought you'd have to go to school)? Why?

You may want to ask questions that help students develop specific parts of their responses, such as the hook and the personal connection.

Step 5: A round of applause

Give your actors a round of applause.

Step 6: Scribe or write a prompt response

Refocus on the prompt rather than the enactment for the written response.

Step 7: Self-edit the response

Use the Standing Ovation Checklist for Poetry Prompts.

All My Hard Work... Ruined!

My Brother Ate a Planet
by John Brassey

I confess it was bizarre,
He consumed a couple comets
Then he gobbled up a star.

He was positively peckish
On an eating escapade,
So he slurped a supernova
With a glass of lemonade.

He absorbed the solar system
With extraordinary haste,
For an interstellar supper
Couldn't satisfy his taste.

He progressed with pure precision
As I witnessed with dismay,
How he swallowed in a second
The entire Milky Way.
Soon he guzzled every galaxy
They never stood a chance,
And were powerless to halt
His astronomical advance.

Not a particle was pardoned
In accordance with his plan,
He ingested every object
In a million light-year span.

All the damage he inflicted
I can't possibly reverse,
I should not have chosen candy
For my model universe.

Writing Assignment

Did you ever work hard to build something, make something, or accomplish something only to have it go wrong or be ruined? Write a composition about when you worked so hard. Include the following:

- What did you work hard to accomplish and why did you want to do this?
- What happened to make it go wrong or be ruined?
- If you had the chance to try again, what could you do differently to make everything go right?
- Be sure to include details, reasons, and examples in your response.

From *See It, Be It, Write It: Using Performing Arts to Improve Writing Skills and Test Scores* by Hope Sara Blecher-Sass, Ed.D., & Maryellen Moffitt, copyright © 2010. Free Spirit Publishing Inc., Minneapolis, MN; 800-735-7323; www.freespirit.com. This page may be reproduced for individual, classroom, and small group work only. For other uses, contact www.freespirit.com/company/permissions.cfm.

All My Hard Work . . . Ruined!

Step 1: Show the prompt

Read the prompt once, including the writing task at the end of the poem, then give students two minutes to reread it and think about it.

All My Hard Work . . . Ruined!

My Brother Ate a Planet
by John Brassey

I confess it was bizarre,
He consumed a couple comets
Then he gobbled up a star.

He was positively peckish
On an eating escapade,
So he slurped a supernova
With a glass of lemonade.

He absorbed the solar system
With extraordinary haste,
For an interstellar supper
Couldn't satisfy his taste.

He progressed with pure precision
As I witnessed with dismay,
How he swallowed in a second
The entire Milky Way.
Soon he guzzled every galaxy
They never stood a chance,
And were powerless to halt
His astronomical advance.

Not a particle was pardoned
In accordance with his plan,
He ingested every object
In a million light-year span.

All the damage he inflicted
I can't possibly reverse,
I should not have chosen candy
For my model universe.

Writing Assignment
Did you ever work hard to build something, make something, or accomplish something only to have it go wrong or be ruined? Write a composition about when you worked so hard. Include the following:

- What did you work hard to accomplish and why did you want to do this?
- What happened to make it go wrong or be ruined?
- If you had the chance to try again, what could you do differently to make everything go right?
- Be sure to include details, reasons, and examples in your response.

Step 2: Discuss the prompt

Have a class discussion about who and what students see in their mental images of the poem and how they might answer the writing task questions. Help them think about personal connections they can make to the poem, including text-to-self, text-to-text, or text-to-world connections. Ask questions to help the brainstorming:

- What is the title of the poem?
- Who is the author of the poem?
- Are you familiar with other poems by John Brassey?
- Who are the characters in the poem?
- How do the characters know each other?
- Where are the kids in this poem? What is the setting (time and location) of the scene?
- What are the kids doing?
- What problem do the siblings have?
- What is a possible solution to the problem?
- Have you ever worked hard on a project only to have something go wrong at the very end?
- How did you feel?
- How did you resolve the situation?
- What could you do to make sure something similar doesn't happen with another project?

Step 3: Enact the prompt

Here are suggestions for how students could approach the enactment.

1. Have students play the roles of the two siblings in the poem and enact two scenes: in the first, one student builds the project, and in the second, the brother (or sister) eats it or otherwise ruins it.

2. Let the second scene play out a bit longer so that the first sibling gets upset about the project being ruined. The two siblings then have to work out a solution to the problem.

3. Students might also enact a personal experience they had when they worked hard on a project or an assignment and something went wrong at the end.

Step 4: Discuss the enactment

Consider the following discussion questions:

- How do you think the person felt when all of his or her work was ruined?
- Do you think the brother was sorry for ruining it? Why or why not?
- What would you do if all your work was ruined prior to an assignment date?
- Would you feel differently if you had time to rebuild the project?
- What are possible ways that work could be ruined just before it is finished? How could you prevent this from happening?

You may want to ask questions that help students develop specific parts of their responses, such as the hook and the personal connection.

Step 5: A round of applause

Give your actors a round of applause.

Step 6: Scribe or write a prompt response

Refocus on the prompt rather than the enactment for the written response.

Step 7: Self-edit the response

Use the Standing Ovation Checklist for Poetry Prompts.

Self Determination

"One of the greatest things you have in life is that no one has the authority to tell you what you want to be. You're the one who'll decide what you want to be."
—*Jaime Escalante, educator*

Write an essay explaining what this quotation means to you. What connections can you make to the meaning of this quote? Use details and examples from your experiences in your composition.

Use the space below for brainstorming.

Self Determination

Step 1: Show the prompt

Read the prompt once, including the writing task at the end of the quote, then give students two minutes to reread it and think about it.

Self Determination

"One of the greatest things you have in life is that no one has the authority to tell you what you want to be. You're the one who'll decide what you want to be."
—*Jaime Escalante, educator*

Write an essay explaining what this quotation means to you. What connections can you make to the meaning of this quote? Use details and examples from your experiences in your composition.

Step 2: Discuss the prompt

Have a class discussion about what students think the quote means and how it might apply to their lives. Help them think about personal connections they can make to the quote, including text-to-self, text-to-text, or text-to-world connections. Ask questions to help the brainstorming:

- To whom is this quote or adage attributed?
- Are you familiar with this person?
- What do you know about this person?
- Have you ever heard or read this quote before?
- What does this quote mean?
- Why might someone try to tell you what you want to be?

Step 3: Enact the prompt

Here are suggestions for how students could approach the enactment.

1. Have students enact various jobs, careers, or goals they have. If students have the same or similar goals, they can enact together.
2. Have one student state what he or she wants to be, then have a few other classmates tell that student he or she has to be something else. Each time the student asserts what he or she wants, the other classmates say otherwise.

3. For an interesting twist on the enactment, have a group of students enact the building of a time machine. One student describes how it works, one student operates the machine, and a few students enter the machine one at a time and exit twenty years older. After exiting the machine in the future, the "older" students describe how their lives have turned out. What do they do every day? Are they happy? Why or why not?

Step 4: Discuss the enactment

Consider the following discussion questions:

- What were some of the more interesting goals or careers enacted? What made them interesting?
- What do you want to be when you grow up? Why?
- What do you think it will take to attain this goal? What obstacles might there be?
- Are you willing to do whatever it takes to attain your goal?
- Do you know anyone else who has this job, career, or aspiration?
- Can that person be a mentor for you? Why or why not?
- How would it feel to be twenty years older than you are today?
- Has anyone ever tried to tell you what to be or do? How does that feel?

You may want to ask questions that help students develop specific parts of their responses, such as the hook and the personal connection.

Step 5: A round of applause

Give your actors a round of applause.

Step 6: Scribe or write a prompt response

Refocus on the prompt rather than the enactment for the written response.

Step 7: Self-edit the response

Use the Standing Ovation Checklist for Quote or Adage Prompts.

Peer Pressure

"It takes a great deal of courage to stand up to your enemies, but even more to stand up to your friends."
—*J.K. Rowling, author (attritubed to the character Albus Dumbledore in her novel* Harry Potter and the Sorcerer's Stone)

Write an essay explaining what this quotation means to you. Explain whether you agree or disagree with this quotation, and why. Use details and examples from your experiences.

Use the space below for brainstorming.

Peer Pressure

Step 1: Show the prompt

Read the prompt once, including the writing task at the end of the quote, then give students two minutes to reread it and think about it.

> ### Peer Pressure
>
> "It takes a great deal of courage to stand up to your enemies, but even more to stand up to your friends."
> —*J.K. Rowling, author (attributed to the character Albus Dumbledore in her novel* Harry Potter and the Sorcerer's Stone*)*
>
> Write an essay explaining what this quotation means to you. Explain whether you agree or disagree with this quotation, and why. Use details and examples from your experiences.

Step 2: Discuss the prompt

Have a class discussion about what students think the quote means and how it might apply to their lives. Help them think about personal connections they can make to the quote, including text-to-self, text-to-text, or text-to-world connections. Ask questions to help the brainstorming:

- To whom is this quote or adage attributed?
- Are you familiar with this person?
- What do you know about J.K. Rowling?
- Have you ever heard or read this quote before?
- What does this quote mean?
- Was there ever a time when your friends asked you to do something you weren't comfortable doing?
- What did they ask you to do?
- Why did you feel uncomfortable?
- Where were you when this occurred?
- If your friends tried to change your mind, what did they do?

Director's Note
Remind students not to use classmates' names during this discussion. 🎭

Step 3: Enact the prompt

Here are suggestions for how students could approach the enactment.

1. Have students enact a scene in which two or more students pressure a friend to let them copy homework. Inject variables into the scenario to see if results will change. For example, in one scenario the friends went to the movies the night before while the other student stayed home doing the work. In another scenario, they worked on the assignment but had trouble with it and weren't able to finish. You can also vary how close the friends are to each other: Would the student let a good buddy copy but not a more casual friend?

2. Consider various other age-appropriate scenarios involving peer pressure.

Step 4: Discuss the enactment

Consider the following discussion questions:

- Did the peer pressure work to change the student's mind? Why or why not?
- If you were in the same situation as the student in the enactment, would you make the same decision? Why or why not?
- How do you think it felt to be the person being pressured?
- How did it feel to be one of the students doing the pressuring?
- What might be some consequences of saying no to friends?
- What about consequences of saying yes?
- Are you good at standing up for what you believe in? How do you know?

You may want to ask questions that help students develop specific parts of their responses, such as the hook and the personal connection.

Step 5: A round of applause

Give your actors a round of applause.

Step 6: Scribe or write a prompt response

Refocus on the prompt rather than the enactment for the written response.

Step 7: Self-edit the response

Use the Standing Ovation Checklist for Quote or Adage Prompts.

Pride

"I like to see a man proud of the place in which he lives. I like to see a man live so that his places will be proud of him."
—*Abraham Lincoln, 16th President of the United States*

Write an essay explaining what this quotation means to you. Explain whether you believe that students can make a difference in a community. Include details and examples from your experiences.

Use the space below for brainstorming.

Pride

Step 1: Show the prompt

Read the prompt once, including the writing task at the end of the quote, then give students two minutes to reread it and think about it.

> ### Pride
>
> "I like to see a man proud of the place in which he lives. I like to see a man live so that his places will be proud of him."
> —*Abraham Lincoln, 16th President of the United States*
>
> Write an essay explaining what this quotation means to you. Explain whether you believe that students can make a difference in a community. Include details and examples from your experiences.

Step 2: Discuss the prompt

Have a class discussion about what students think the quote means and how it might apply to their lives. Help them think about personal connections they can make to the quote, including text-to-self, text-to-text, or text-to-world connections. Ask questions to help the brainstorming:

- To whom is this quote or adage attributed?
- Are you familiar with Abraham Lincoln?
- What do you know about this person?
- Have you ever heard or read this quote before?
- What does this quote mean?
- How would you describe your community?
- What is your community known for?
- Why are you proud of your community?
- Has anyone famous lived in your community? Who was it? What was that person known for?
- Is there anything historical that happened in your area? What?
- What makes you feel like you are part of your community?
- What do you do that makes your community proud of you? Or what could you do to make your community proud of you?

Step 3: Enact the prompt

Here are suggestions for how students could approach the enactment.

1. Have students enact a mock interview in which one student is the reporter for a newspaper or Web site and a few other students have worked together to perform an act of community service. Students should be sure to describe the act of community service they did and why the town members are so proud of them.

2. Alternatively, have students enact the community service itself. Consider doing before and after scenarios, where they enact a problem or situation that needs solving and then enact the community service that addresses the problem.

3. Have students enact a great moment happening in a community, such as a teacher winning teacher of the year or a local team winning a big game.

Step 4: Discuss the enactment

Consider the following discussion questions:

- How do you think the people involved in the community service or great community moment felt?
- Have you ever done something similar to this? If so, what was it? How did it feel? If not, what would you like to do? Why?
- Do you believe that kids can make a positive difference in their town? Why or why not?
- What community service project would you like to do in the future, and why?
- In what ways could a community recognize kids who make positive contributions to the community?

You may want to ask questions that help students develop specific parts of their responses, such as the hook and the personal connection.

Step 5: A round of applause

Give your actors a round of applause.

Step 6: Scribe or write a prompt response

Refocus on the prompt rather than the enactment for the written response.

Step 7: Self-edit the response

Use the Standing Ovation Checklist for Quote or Adage Prompts.

Believe in Yourself

"Some people say that I have an attitude. Maybe I do. But I think that you have to. You have to believe in yourself when no one else does—that makes you a winner right there."
—*Venus Williams, professional tennis player*

Write an essay explaining what this quotation means to you. Explain whether you agree or disagree with this quotation. Use details and examples from your experiences.

Use the space below for brainstorming.

Believe in Yourself

Step 1: Show the prompt

Read the prompt once, including the writing task at the end of the quote, then give students two minutes to reread it and think about it.

> ### Believe in Yourself
>
> "Some people say that I have an attitude. Maybe I do. But I think that you have to. You have to believe in yourself when no one else does—that makes you a winner right there."
> —*Venus Williams, professional tennis player*
>
> Write an essay explaining what this quotation means to you. Explain whether you agree or disagree with this quotation. Use details and examples from your experiences.

Step 2: Discuss the prompt

Have a class discussion about what students think the quote means and how it might apply to their lives. Help them think about personal connections they can make to the quote, including text-to-self, text-to-text, or text-to-world connections. Ask questions to help the brainstorming:

- To whom is this quote or adage attributed?
- Are you familiar with Venus Williams?
- What do you know about her?
- Have you ever heard or read this quote before?
- What does this quote mean?
- What are you good at?
- How did you become good at it?
- What does being confident feel like?
- Is your confidence consistent? Do you remain confident when things are difficult or an opponent is better than you?
- How do you remain confident when you face challenges/challengers?
- What are positive and negative meanings of the word "attitude"?

Step 3: Enact the prompt

Here are suggestions for how students could approach the enactment.

1. Have students enact a competition of some kind, such as a spelling bee. For the spelling bee scenario, you might have three judges, the word announcer, the score keeper, and the two finalists. During the spell-off, two students prove that they have equal ability, but as the pressure increases, one student begins to act nervous while the other remains confident.

2. In a similar enactment, have one student who begins to do poorly in the contest or game but clearly maintains a positive, self-confident attitude. Perhaps the winning contestant tries to intimidate the other or brag, displaying a negative attitude. But the first contestant believes in herself no matter what, displaying a positive attitude.

Step 4: Discuss the enactment

Consider the following discussion questions:

- Do you think it was hard for the actor to keep a positive attitude?
- What role does confidence play during competition? Does it make any difference? If so, what?
- How does it feel to compete against someone else who has confidence?
- What can you do to help yourself build confidence?
- What could you do to help a friend build confidence?
- Does confidence only come from being the best? Why or why not?
- Can you ever feel too confident? If so, how or why? What does it meant to be too confident?
- Has that ever happened to you or someone you know?
- What makes a person lose confidence? Can confidence be regained?

You may want to ask questions that help students develop specific parts of their responses, such as the hook and the personal connection.

Step 5: A round of applause

Give your actors a round of applause.

Step 6: Scribe or write a prompt response

Refocus on the prompt rather than the enactment for the written response.

Step 7: Self-edit the response

Use the Standing Ovation Checklist for Quote or Adage Prompts.

Taking a Risk

"A person who never made a mistake never tried anything new."
—*Albert Einstein, scientist*

Write an essay explaining what this quotation means to you. Explain how this connects to your experiences. Use details and examples from your experiences.

Use the space below for brainstorming.

Taking a Risk

Step 1: Show the prompt

Read the prompt once, including the writing task at the end of the quote, then give students two minutes to reread it and think about it.

Taking a Risk

"A person who never made a mistake never tried anything new."
—*Albert Einstein, scientist*

Write an essay explaining what this quotation means to you. Explain how this connects to your experiences. Use details and examples from your experiences.

Step 2: Discuss the prompt

Have a class discussion about what students think the quote means and how it might apply to their lives. Help them think about personal connections they can make to the quote, including text-to-self, text-to-text, or text-to-world connections. Ask questions to help the brainstorming:

- To whom is this quote or adage attributed?
- Are you familiar with Albert Einstein?
- What do you know about him?
- Have you ever heard or read this quote before?
- What does this quote mean?
- What new thing have you tried to learn?
- Why did you want to learn it?
- Was it easy or difficult to learn? Why?
- How long did it take to learn it?
- Did you feel discouraged? If so, did you keep trying? Why or why not?
- How did you feel when you made mistakes?

Step 3: Enact the prompt

Here are suggestions for how students could approach the enactment.

1. Have students enact learning to do something difficult. Perhaps they can remember what it was like learning to ride a bicycle or skateboard or to ice skate. Perhaps they will enact something academic, such as learning a difficult math concept. Have students enact being excited about learning the new skill but having difficulty, perhaps failing multiple times before finally succeeding.

2. As an extension of #1, show other kids successfully doing the activity that the other students can't learn. The first student might get frustrated and give up or keep trying. The other students might try to help.

3. Consider having students enact a time they tried to learn something but ultimately gave up or were not able to learn it. Is it okay not to succeed at something? Is there anything to learn from failure?

Step 4: Discuss the enactment

Consider the following discussion questions:

- How do you think it felt for the person to struggle to learn?
- Were the other kids supportive? How do you know?
- Did that make a difference?
- Is it harder or easier when you can see other kids your age doing it? Why?
- What would have happened if the person had not attempted to learn to ride the bicycle (or skateboard, etc.)?
- What can you learn from struggling to do something as opposed to doing it easily?
- What advice would you give to someone trying to learn the same thing?
- What new thing would you like to try? Why?

You may want to ask questions that help students develop specific parts of their responses, such as the hook and the personal connection.

Step 5: A round of applause

Give your actors a round of applause.

Step 6: Scribe or write a prompt response

Refocus on the prompt rather than the enactment for the written response.

Step 7: Self-edit the response

Use the Standing Ovation Checklist for Quote or Adage Prompts.

Baseball

Themed Prompt Set

All prompts available as student reproducible handouts on the CD-ROM.

Picture prompt

A picture tells a story.
Write a story that brings this picture to life.

Speculative prompt

The brother and sister knew that one day they would be on opposing teams, but they never thought it would be in the championship game. To top it off, their dad is the umpire. It's the bottom of the ninth inning, there are two outs, and the score is tied. Mom is sitting in the bleachers. She doesn't know which child to root for, the one at bat or the one who's the catcher.

- Write a story about the mom, her situation, and how it is resolved.
- Be sure to include details in your response.

Persuasive prompt

Recently, a student at your school broke her arm playing baseball during gym. It was a freak accident, but now a group of parents at your school is trying to get baseball eliminated from gym class so no one else will be hurt. The gym teachers say baseball is a fun and important sport. Your principal has to decide.

Write a letter to your principal arguing for or against the idea of eliminating baseball from gym. Make sure to support your stance with reasons and details.

Poetry prompt

Read the poem "The New Kid" by Mike Makley (find it by searching at www.baseball-almanac.com) to students. Provide the following writing assignment.

Was it a surprise to find out the new kid was a girl? Why? Write about a time you were surprised by how well someone did or a time you surprised others by how well you did. Be sure to include examples and details in your response.

Quote prompt

"The way a team plays as a whole determines its success. You may have the greatest bunch of individual stars in the world, but if they don't play together, the club won't be worth a dime."
—*Babe Ruth, baseball player*

Write an essay explaining what this quote means to you. Explain how it relates to a team or group you have been a part of, either in sports, school, or somewhere else. Be sure to use details and examples from your experience.

Extensions

Gifted and talented: Have students invent a new game, complete with a set of rules, and incorporate this new game into a story. Or have them listen to "Who's on First" by Abbott and Costello and create a flow chart that corresponds with the verses.

Special needs: Have students work in small groups to enact a favorite sport and write a story about playing.

English language learners: Have students mime one at-bat or one inning of a baseball game or another sport. This is especially useful as a prewriting activity for students from a country or culture where baseball—and baseball terminology—are unfamiliar.

Visual/artistic connection: Have students create a team logo or uniform or a banner or flyer announcing a game.

Musical connection: Have students enact or sing your country's national anthem or "Take Me Out to the Ballgame" and write a story about a singer performing at a high-pressure playoff game.

Social-emotional connection: Have students enact helping a friend after his or her play causes the team to lose an important game. Students write a speculative response or personal story about what they would do in this situation. Or have students read or listen to "Casey at the Bat" by Ernest Thayer and write about a similar experience.

Technology connection: Video record an enactment of a close play in a game and use the video as a prop in enacting an instant replay analysis.

A picture tells a story.
Write a story that brings this picture to life.

Lemonade

All prompts available as student reproducible handouts on the CD-ROM.

Picture prompt

A picture tells a story.
Write a story that brings this picture to life.

Speculative prompt

A brother and sister have been planning all week to have a lemonade stand on Saturday. When the day finally arrives, they make their lemonade and begin to set up the stand. Suddenly dark clouds appear in the sky. In moments, it is pouring rain.

- Write a story about the lemonade sale.
- Be sure to include details in your response.

Persuasive prompt

Last summer, you set up a lemonade stand in front of your home and had a lot of fun while making a little money. You want to do it again this year, but the mayor is considering a rule that would prohibit selling lemonade because lemonade is sugary and unhealthy. The rule would be part of the mayor's new "Healthy Living" campaign.

Write a letter to your mayor arguing for or against this new rule. Make sure to support your stance with reasons and details.

Poetry prompt

Read the poem "Dreaming of Summer" by Kenn Nesbitt (find it by searching at www.poetry4kids.com) to students. Provide the following writing assignment.

Think about a time you were daydreaming because you did not want to do what you had to do at that moment. Write about how daydreaming made you feel. Be sure to include examples and details in your response.

Quote prompt

"When life gives you lemons, you make lemonade. I have several stands around here."
—*James Brady, politician and activist*

In this quote, James Brady is talking about making the best of a bad thing. Write an essay explaining what this quote means to you. Explain how it relates to something that has happened to you. Be sure to use details and examples from your experience.

Extensions

Gifted and talented: Have students write about a lemonade stand transaction in which a dissatisfied customer demands a refund. Have the students incorporate dialogue into their writing.

Special needs: Have students work in pairs or small groups to enact a transaction at the lemonade stand. Set a price for the lemonade and have students pay and make change. Consider having them draw and cut out pieces of money.

English language learners: To help students gain vocabulary, have them look at real lemonade-related items (or images of the items) and draw a lemonade stand, including people selling and buying lemonade, and label parts as appropriate, such as *pitcher, cup, glass, table, customer, boy, girl, lemon, lemonade, ice,* and so on.

Visual/artistic connection: Have students create flyers or posters advertising a lemonade stand. This can be a form of persuasive writing, as the flyer persuades readers to buy lemonade.

Musical connection: Have students write and perform a lemonade stand jingle or advertisement. This is a form of persuasive writing, persuading people to buy lemonade.

Social-emotional connection: Add a moral dilemma to the enactment and writing assignment, such as a thirsty child who does not have enough money for lemonade.

Technology connection: Video record an enactment of a rain storm wrecking a lemonade stand, and have students add music and sound effects, such as wind and thunder.

A picture tells a story.

Write a story that brings this picture to life.

Recycling

All prompts available as student reproducible handouts on the CD-ROM.

Picture prompt

A picture tells a story.
Write a story that brings this picture to life.

Speculative prompt

You are at a party with friends, and you're having a great time. But you notice that plastic bottles and aluminum cans are being thrown in the garbage instead of being recycled.

- Write a story about what happens next.
- Be sure to include details in your response.

Persuasive prompt

The company that provides lunches to your school uses Styrofoam containers, which are dangerous to the environment, and the company does not recycle any materials they use. Your school is considering changing to a new lunch provider that does recycle, but this change would cause the cost of lunch to go up.

Write a letter to your principal arguing for or against this change. Make sure to support your stance with reasons and details.

Poetry prompt

Read the poem "Sarah Cynthia Sylvia Stout Would Not Take the Garbage Out" by Shel Silverstein (from *Where the Sidewalk Ends*, 1974, and available as an audio recording released in 1983; search for it at lyricsplayground.com) to students. Provide the following writing assignment.

Why do you think Sarah refused to take out the garbage? What were the consequences of her actions? Write about a time you refused to do something and it didn't turn out well. Be sure to include examples and details in your response.

Quote prompt

"Just as we cannot blame others for destroying the environment, so we cannot look to others to protect the environment. Responsibility for both begins at home."
—*Paul Griss, conservationist*

Explain how this quote about responsibility relates to you. What is something you and your family take responsibility for? Be sure to use details and examples from your experience.

Extensions

Gifted and talented: Have students write a story that follows a piece of garbage that does not get recycled, from the moment it is used until its final stop. Then have them write another story that follows a piece of garbage that is recycled. Finally, have them write a paragraph comparing the two journeys. How are they different and the same?

Special needs: As developmentally appropriate, have students work in pairs and with you to illustrate the poem and explore its meaning. Students may record their voices reciting the poem.

English language learners: Have students share information about recycling in their home countries. Tour the school to locate recycling containers. Have students mime or act out the recycling process.

Visual/artistic connection: Have students create posters to encourage other students to recycle. Hang the posters throughout the school. These can be a form of persuasive writing as students build arguments persuading others to recycle.

Musical connection: Have students write and perform a song about recycling and perform it for other students, who then write a poetry prompt response.

Social-emotional connection: Give students the following writing assignment.

As part of a "Going Green" theme, your school is holding a contest: the homeroom that recycles the most wins a pizza party that includes a visit by a celebrity. One of your friends does not recycle and thinks recycling is a waste of time. Your classmates have asked you to talk to your friend to get him to join the cause. Write a story about what you do.

Technology connection: Have students use Microsoft Publisher or a similar design program to create a recycling newsletter for your classroom, grade, or school. Have them include photographs, stories, poetry, persuasive letters—even original research.

A picture tells a story.
Write a story that brings this picture to life.

Shoes

All prompts available as student reproducible handouts on the CD-ROM.

Picture prompt

A picture tells a story.
Write a story that brings this picture to life.

Speculative prompt

On the way home from his friend's house, Sanjay discovers a pair of brand new sneakers under a bush, and they are just the kind he has been wanting. To his surprise, when he tries them on, he discovers they give him a magical ability.

- Write a story about what happens next. What is the magical ability and what does Sanjay do with it?
- Be sure to include details in your response.

Persuasive prompt

You are shopping for school clothes with your father when you see a pair of sneakers you really want. But before you can even ask for them, your father cuts you off by saying no. The sneakers are too expensive, and you have other clothes you need more, like pants and a new jacket.

    Write a letter to your father arguing for the shoes. Make sure to support your argument with reasons and details.

Poetry prompt

Read the lyrics from the song "New Shoes" by Paolo Nutini (do a search on www.absolutelyrics.com) to students. Play the song, if possible. Provide the following writing assignment.

    In the song "New Shoes," the singer feels great wearing new shoes. Write about a time you got something new and felt great. What did you get? Why did it make you feel so good? Be sure to include examples and details in your response.

Quote prompt

"These are my new shoes. They're good shoes. They won't make you rich like me, they won't make you rebound like me, they definitely won't make you handsome like me. They'll only make you have shoes like me. That's it."
—*Charles Barkley, basketball star*

In this quote, Charles Barkley is talking about his signature shoes. Why do you think people want to be like sports stars or other celebrities? Who is a famous person you admire? Do you want to be like him or her? Why? Write an essay explaining how this quote relates to you. Be sure to use details and examples from your experience.

Extensions

Gifted and talented: Have students research the shoe size tool used in shoe stores and invent a new tool to measure shoe size. Have them write a story about their invention.

Special needs: Depending on ability levels, pair older students with younger students and have them show their younger buddy how to tie shoelaces or buckle shoes. Students may audio or video record their demonstration so that the younger students can use it as a learning center activity.

English language learners: Have students learn vocabulary by researching shoes and making a poster showing different types of shoes, from sandals to snow boots, and labeling each image. Posters could also include shoes from different countries.

Visual/artistic connection: Have students create an advertisement for a pair of sneakers, and, using the ad as a visual aid, write a persuasive essay urging readers to choose these shoes. Have them send their advertisements to the shoe company.

Musical connection: Have students create a piece of music based on the sounds of shoes clicking against pavement, stones, or tiles.

Social-emotional connection: Read the short story "The Sound of Summer Running" by Ray Bradbury and discuss the change in attitude of the two characters.

Technology connection: Have students research the evolution of sneakers or tennis shoes and/or conduct a survey of students and staff regarding favorite shoe styles and colors. Then have them create a PowerPoint presentation to show their results. The presentation should include images and analysis, perhaps including graphs and tables.

A picture tells a story.

Write a story that brings this picture to life.

Hard-Knock Life

All prompts available as student reproducible handouts on the CD-ROM.

Picture prompt

A picture tells a story.
Write a story that brings this picture to life.

Speculative prompt

A brother and sister have been asked by a parent to clean the kitchen. That means doing the dishes, scrubbing the counters and floor, and washing the inside of the oven, microwave, and refrigerator. They also have to take out the garbage. Just as they are getting started, two friends come to the door wanting to play outside.

- Write a story about what happens next. What will the brother and sister do?
- Be sure to include details in your response.

Persuasive prompt

You do chores at home in order to earn an allowance, but you don't feel you are paid fairly for the work you do.

Decide whether you would rather be paid more allowance or have fewer chores, then write a letter to a parent arguing your position. Make sure to support your argument with reasons and details.

Poetry prompt

Read the lyrics from the song "It's the Hard-Knock Life" from the Broadway show *Annie* (search for lyrics at www.allmusicals.com) to students. Play the song, if possible. Provide the following writing assignment.

In the song "It's the Hard-Knock Life," the kids sing about their difficult life. Why do they consider their lives to be hard? Write an essay about the hardest part of your life. Be sure to include examples and details in your response.

Quote prompt

"I always thought a yard was three feet, then I started mowing the lawn."
—*C.E. Cowman*

Think of a time when a task ended up being much harder or bigger than you thought it would be. Write an essay explaining what the task was and what you did. Be sure to use details and examples from your experience.

Extensions

Gifted and talented: Have students talk with a custodian to see how long it takes to mop one classroom, then calculate how long it takes to mop all the classrooms in the school. Have them calculate times for the gym and lunchroom, too.

Special needs: Organize an opportunity for students to meet with a member of the custodial staff to learn about the tools they use in their job. Then have students write a brief report or create a drawing or collage that describes the tools and what they are used for. Students may work alone or in pairs or teams.

English language learners: Have students create a list of words related to cleaning and chores and define them. Then have them write a brief story or descriptive paragraph about a chore using the words. Finally, have them paste the text of their story into a word cloud tool such as www.wordle.net.

Visual/artistic connection: Have students create a collage of images representing chores or challenges that are difficult to do along with tools that make those things easier. For example, a messy floor and a mop or a snowy sidewalk and a snow shovel.

Musical connection: Have students create or find background music for enactments that would speed up or slow down the cleaning or affect the moods of the participants. They could change the words to "It's the Hard-Knock Life" to better reflect the students' lives.

Social-emotional connection: Add a moral dilemma to the enactment and writing assignment, such as a child who refuses to help do the work. What would the students say to this person?

Technology connection: Create a podcast in which students sing "It's the Hard-Knock Life" and read their written responses. Put a link to the podcast in your Twitter feed and ask for comments from other teachers and classrooms.

A picture tells a story.
Write a story that brings this picture to life.

References and Resources

BrainyQuote (www.brainyquote.com). This is a rich source for quotes by past and current people from a variety of walks of life. It is easy to search and user friendly.

CASEL: Collaborative for Academic Social and Emotional Learning (www.casel.org). A leading advocate for establishing social-emotional learning (SEL) as an essential part of education. Their Web site provides basic guidelines for SEL, answers FAQs, and provides resources for educators.

Critical Evidence: How the Arts Benefit Student Achievement. Sandra S. Ruppert. National Assembly of State Art Agencies and Arts Education Partnership, 2006 (www.nasaa-arts .org). Why is it so important to keep the arts strong in our schools? How does the study of the arts contribute to student achievement and success? These questions and other important information are addressed in this downloadable booklet.

Differentiated Instructional Strategies: One Size Doesn't Fit All. Carolyn Chapman and Gale H. Gregory. Thousand Oaks, CA: Corwin Press, 2007. Features practical techniques and processes that teachers can use to adjust learning based on individual students' knowledge, skills, experience, preferences, and needs.

Differentiating Instruction in the Regular Classroom: How to Reach and Teach All Learners, Grades 3-12. Diane Heacox. Minneapolis: Free Spirit Publishing Inc., 2002. This guide offers a menu of strategies, examples, templates, and tools teachers can use to differentiate instruction in any curriculum, and it works especially well with differentiating the enactment/writing process.

Education World (www.educationworld.com). This Web site provides educators with lesson plans, professional development, and help for integrating technology into the classroom. You can also access national and state education standards here.

Georgia Department of Education (www.doe .k12.ga.us). Use this site to find writing assessments, rubrics, and released test items beginning with kindergarten and advancing through high school.

Hear! Here! Sounds Around the World. Michele Slung. New York: Crown Publishing Group, 1994. This book is the source for onomatopoeias in various languages. Use it to invite students to share their vocabulary and to make global connections fit into their oral and written stories.

Illinois Learning Standards for Social-Emotional Learning (SEL) (www.isbe.net/ils/ social_emotional/standards.htm). Illinois is at the forefront of specifically stating standards for social and emotional learning for students in grades K through 12. At this Web site readers will find standards, descriptors, and resources.

Imagine: The Spirit of American Heroes. Gina Misiroglu. Novato, CA: New World Library, 1999. Useful for cross-curricular connections, and picture and quote prompts, this book includes photographs, quotations, and information about an array of people and their place in history.

Massachusetts Department of Elementary and Secondary Education (www.doe.mass .edu). Massachusetts is one of the states that releases test items to the public after students have completed the assessment period. Viewers can see examples of previous tests, students' responses, and a question of the day.

Napster (www.napster.com). Search for and download songs (for a fee) that can be used as writing prompts.

National Baseball Hall of Fame (www .baseballhall.org). The National Baseball Hall of Fame has a section on its Web site for educators. Teachers and sports aficionados can find information about field trips, video conferences, and thematic lessons.

The National Standards for Arts Education (artsedge.kennedy-center.org/teach/standards). This Web site lists the standards that outline what every K–12 student should know and be able to do in the arts, including dance, music, theater, and the visual arts.

New Jersey Department of Education (www .state.nj.us/education). Students, parents, and educators will find FAQs, documents, and PowerPoints with information about the curriculum standards and the state assessments at this Web site.

North Carolina Department of Education (www.dpi.state.nc.us/accountability). North Carolina is one of the states that releases test items to the public after students have completed the assessment period. Visitors will find examples of previous tests, assessment result reports, and links to state and national assessment programs.

Poetry Foundation (www.poetryfoundation .org). The Poetry Foundation is the publisher of Poetry magazine as well as a Web site that contains a "poetry tool," a large database of poems searchable by title, poet, first line, and other ways. A great resource for poetry prompts.

Projects & Presentations for K–6 Students: Preparing Kids to Be Confident, Effective Communicators. Phil Schlemmer and Dori Schlemmer. Minneapolis: Free Spirit Publishing Inc., 2009. This book helps students master the skills of oral presentation in an engaging, differentiated, project-based way. Strategies and projects are presented to help students become effective communicators and self-directed learners while offering the freedom to be unique.

Songfacts (www.songfacts.com). Songfacts provides song lyrics and suggested songs according to topic. Great source for selecting songs to be used as writing prompts.

Strategies for Differentiating Instruction: Best Practices for the Classroom. Julia L. Roberts and Tracy F. Inman. Waco, TX: Prufrock Press, 2007. This book provides practical strategies that allow all students to learn at appropriately challenging levels and make continuous progress by focusing on their various levels of knowledge and readiness to learn. The strategies serve as an easy-to-use foundation for differentiating the enactment/writing process.

Swimming Upstream. Kristine O'Connell George. New York: Houghton Mifflin Company, 2002. This book includes poems for kids that will make them smile, laugh, and reflect upon life in school from homework to lockers, band to lunch.

Teaching Beyond the Test: Differentiated Project-Based Learning in a Standards-Based Age, Grades 6 & Up. Phil Schlemmer and Dori Schlemmer. Minneapolis: Free Spirit Publishing Inc., 2008. This book helps students meet curriculum benchmarks while being challenged to learn more than just how to take tests. This resource presents proven strategies for differentiation and a dozen projects that model the strategies.

Teaching Gifted Kids in the Regular Classroom: Strategies and Techniques Every Teacher Can Use to Meet the Academic Needs of the Gifted and Talented. Susan Winebrenner. Minneapolis: Free Spirit Publishing Inc., 2001. This is a definitive guide to meeting the learning needs of gifted students in the mixed abilities classroom. It's full of proven, practical, classroom-tested strategies teachers love. The differentiation techniques may be easily applied during writing instruction and test preparation.

Testing Miss Malarkey. Judy Finchler. New York: Walker Publishing Company, 2000. This is a book students and teachers enjoy year after year. It puts the high stakes testing situation into both a fun and understandable context. Perfect for sharing at PTA/PTO meetings, too.

Texas Education Agency (www.tea.state.tx.us). Viewers will find information about the Texas Essential Knowledge and Skills curriculum standards (TEKS) and the Texas Assessment of Knowledge and Skills (TAKS). Online interactive versions of the tests are available in English and Spanish.

Vincent's Colors. Vincent van Gogh and the Metropolitan Museum of Art. San Francisco: Chronicle Books, 2005. Throughout this book, various van Gogh paintings are partnered with text taken from letters that Vincent wrote to his brother, Theo. This visual textual book makes his works accessible to learners of all ages, children through adult.

Index

A

Accommodations, 35
Adage prompts, *See* Quote or adage prompts
Adjectives and adverbs, 32
All My Hard Work . . . Ruined! (poetry prompt), 156–157
"American Icon" thematic unit, 111
Anchor activities, 60
Anxiety, performance and test-taking, 68–69
Apology methodology activity, 72–73
Argumentative writing, *See* Persuasive prompts
Arts education content standards, 9, 179
Assessments
    accommodations, 35
    authentic writing prompts, 43–45
    handwriting and erasing in, 34–35
    scoring, 2, 28, 33
    "stop" versus "end" instructions, 34
    test preparation tips, 45–46
    test-taking anxiety, 69
    writing for, 1–2, 28
    See also State standards and assessments
Assessment Writing Clusters chart, 11, 14
Audience
    roles, 19, 69
    seating, 62–63

B

Baseball theme, 58, 79–81, 168–169, 178
Being Part of a Family (poetry prompt), 148–149
Believe in Yourself (quote or adage prompt), 164–165
Benchmarks, *See* Proficiency levels
A Birthday Superpower Surprise (poetry prompt), 152–153
Brainstorming, 18, 38
BrainyQuote (Web site), 104, 178

C

California, 7–8
CASEL (Collaborative for Academic, Social, and
    Emotional Learning), 68, 178
Characters, naming, 29
Choice-as-motivator activities, 60–61
The Class Pet (speculative prompt), 136–137
Class Progressive Writing Chart, 16
Classroom theaters, 62–64
Coding written responses, 36, 37, 59
Collaborative for Academic, Social, and Emotional
    Learning, 68, 178
Common Core Standards, 6
Compositions, *See* Written responses
Concerned About Curfews (persuasive prompt), 146–147
Conflicts or problems
    including in stories, 30, 33–34
    as indications of student crises, 30
Cool Things You Learn in School (poetry prompt), 150–151
Costumes, 64–65
Cross-curricular activities
    thematic units, 110–111
    writing prompts, 112–116

Cubing, 56–58
Curriculum standards, *See* State standards and assessments

D

Data collection charts
    Assessment Writing Clusters chart, 11, 14
    Class Progressive Writing Chart, 16
    Previous Writing Test Data Collection Sheet, 11, 13
    Student Progressive Writing Chart, 11, 15
    Writing Assessment Information Fact Sheet, 12
Desktop theaters, 65–67
Dialogue, 30–31
Differentiated teaching
    anchor activities, 60
    choice-as-motivator activities, 60–61
    connecting students' strengths, 54
    cubing, 56–58
    flexible grouping, 39, 55–56
    incorporating during the school year, 39–41
    kids teaching kids activities, 41, 58–59
    multiple intelligences, 61
    scaffolding, 55
    tiered assignments, 59
Discussion questions, 21
    See also specific prompt types

E

Editing, 26
Education World (Web site), 9, 43, 178
Emotion commotion
    activity, 72
    cards, 75, 76
Empathy, promoting, 69
Enactment process, *See* Prompt enactment process
Ending punctuation, 31
Energy Saving Schedule (persuasive prompt), 142–143
Erasing, 35
Essays, *See* Written responses
Explanatory/expository writing, *See* Poetry prompts; Quote
    or adage prompts

F

Fan mail, 22
A Favorite Memory (poetry prompt), 154–155
5MOPS strategy, 24–25, 32–33
5 synonym switch, 26, 32
Flexible grouping, 39, 55–56
A Friend in Need (speculative prompt), 132–133

G

Georgia, 44, 178
Grouping students, 39, 41, 55–56, 58–59

H

Handwriting, 34–35
Hard-Knock Life (themed prompt set), 176–177

Hooks, creating, 24, 29–30
"How You Feel About It" cards, 75

I

I found it! Is it mine? activity, 72
Illinois, 70, 71, 178
Indenting paragraphs, 34
Interpersonal skills, *See* Social-emotional learning (SEL)

J

Jargon conversion table, 10
Jeopardy! games, 41

K

Kids teaching kids activities, 41, 58–59

L

Language arts curriculum standards, 7–8
Left is right! activity, 43
Lemonade theme, 18–26, 29–34, 111, 170–171
Letters
    delivering, 96
    fan mail, 22
    format, 91, 94
    See also Persuasive prompts
Lighting effects, 63–64

M

Mary Poppins (movie), 17
Massachusetts, 179
Mastery levels, terminology, 10, 11
Math writing prompts, 112–113
Me? A Winner? (speculative prompt), 134–135
Message in a Bottle (persuasive prompt), 140–141
Metaphors, 24
Modeling, 23–26
Multiple intelligences, 61
Music
    in enactments, 63
    song lyrics as prompts, 73, 115–116, 178, 179

N

Narrative writing, *See* Story components
National Assessment of Educational Progress (NAEP), 28
New Jersey, 35, 44, 45, 179
Nice was eaten by mice activity, 32
North Carolina, 44–45, 179

O

Off Topic (OT) scores, 33
On My Way (picture prompt), 124–125
Onomatopoeia, 24
Oregon, 45

P

Paragraphs, indenting, 34
Peer Pressure (quote or adage prompt), 160–161
Performance anxiety, 68–69
Personification, 24
Persuasive prompts
    authentic samples, 44–45
    delivering letters, 96
    enacting, 89–92
    overview, 10, 88
    playing cards, 49–50
    prompt sources, 44–45, 88
    ready-to-use prompts, 138–147

    Standing Ovation Checklist, 93–95
    writing example, 94–95
Photographs
    of enactment process, 20, 116
    as writing prompts, 71, 78
Physical education writing prompts, 116
Picture prompts
    authentic samples, 44
    enacting, 18–23, 79–81
    overview, 10, 78
    picture sources, 78–79
    playing cards, 47–48
    ready-to-use prompts, 118–127
    Standing Ovation Checklist, 29–35, 82
Playing cards
    how to use, 42–43
    persuasive prompts, 49–50
    picture and speculative prompts, 47–48
    poetry and quote or adage prompts, 51–52
Poetry Foundation (Web site), 179
Poetry prompts
    authentic samples, 45
    enacting, 97–100
    overview, 10, 97
    playing cards, 51–52
    prompt sources, 97
    ready-to-use prompts, 148–157
    Standing Ovation Checklist, 101–103
    writing example, 102–103
Previous Writing Test Data Collection Sheet, 11, 13
Pride (quote or adage prompt), 162–163
Problems, *See* Conflicts or problems
Proficiency levels, terminology, 10, 11
Prompt enactment process
    adjusting during the school year, 38–40
    authentic prompts, using, 43–45
    benefits of, 2–3, 68–69, 71
    first-time suggestions, 17
    social-emotional learning, promoting, 68–71
    steps, 2, 18–23
    types of prompts, 10–11
    See also specific prompt types
Props, 64, 67
Punctuation, 31
Put *said* to bed activity, 31–32

Q

Questions, for class discussion, 21
Quotation marks, 31
Quotationspage.com, 104
Quote or adage prompts
    authentic samples, 45
    enacting, 105–108
    overview, 10–11, 104
    playing cards, 51–52
    prompt sources, 104–105
    ready-to-use prompts, 158–167
    Standing Ovation Checklist, 109

R

Ready to Ride (picture prompt), 122–123
Ready-to-use prompts
    persuasive prompts, 138–147
    picture prompts, 118–127
    poetry prompts, 148–157
    quote or adage prompts, 158–167
    speculative prompts, 128–137

Recycling (themed prompt set), 172–173
Round of applause, 22

S

Said, using synonyms for, 31–32
Scaffolding, 55
Scenery, 63
School Closed (speculative prompt), 130–131
School Improvement Is Up to You (persuasive prompt), 144–145
Science writing prompts, 113–114
Scoring writing assessments, 2, 28, 33
Scribing class responses, 23–26
SEL, *See* Social-emotional learning (SEL)
Self Determination (quote or adage prompt), 158–159
Self-editing, 26
    See also specific prompt types
Self-esteem, *See* Social-emotional learning (SEL)
Selling a Cell Phone (persuasive prompt), 138–139
Senses, encouraging use of, 24
Shoes (themed prompt set), 174–175
Similes, 24
Social-emotional learning (SEL)
    empathy, encouraging, 69
    enactment process and, 68–71
    Illinois goals, standards, and descriptors, 70, 71
    writing prompts, 71–73
Social studies writing prompts, 114
Song lyrics as prompts, 73, 115–116, 178, 179
Speculative prompts
    authentic samples, 44
    enacting, 84–86
    overview, 10, 83
    playing cards, 47–48
    prompt sources, 83–84
    ready-to-use prompts, 128–137
    Standing Ovation Checklist, 29–35, 87
Stage areas, 62–63
Standardized tests, *See* Assessments
Standing Ovation Checklists
    how to use, 35–37
    overview and components, 2, 28–35
    persuasive prompts, 93–95
    picture prompts, 29–35, 82
    playing cards, 42–43, 47–52
    poetry prompts, 101–103
    quote or adage prompts, 109
    speculative prompts, 29–35, 87
    student internalization of, 40–41
State standards and assessments
    alignment with, 3
    Common Core Standards, 6
    determining assessment content, 9–10
    jargon conversion table, 10
    language arts, 7–8
    sample prompts, 44–45
    scoring considerations, 2, 28, 33
    social-emotional learning, 70, 71
    Web sites, 178, 179
Story components, 23–26, 29–35
Student Progressive Writing Chart, 11, 15
Students
    gathering and charting information about, 11, 12–16
    indications of crisis situations, 30
    tapping natural strengths of, 54, 61
    test-taking considerations, 45–46, 68–69
Sunday in the Park with George, 17

The Surprise Outside (speculative prompt), 128–129
Synonyms, use of, 31–32

T

Taking a Risk (quote or adage prompt), 166–167
Teachers
    collaboration, 11, 111
    as scribes, 23
Technology education writing prompts, 116
Techteachers.com, 41
Terminology
    jargon conversion table, 10
    proficiency levels, 10, 11
    "stop" versus "end" instructions, 34
Test day preparation tips, 45–46
Test-taking anxiety, 69
Tests, *See* Assessments
Texas, 7–8, 44, 179
Text, connections to, 20, 32
Theaters
    classrooms as, 62–64
    desktop, 65–67
    See also Prompt enactment process
Theatre content standards, 9
Thematic units
    suggested approach, 110–111
    themed prompt sets, 168–177
Thinkexist.com, 104
Tiered assignments, 59
Timing of assessments, 45–46
Titles, choosing, 25–26, 35
Transitional words, 95, 102

V

Verbs, 32
Visual arts
    content standards, 9
    writing prompts, 114–115
Visual stimuli, *See* Picture prompts
Visualization, 39–40
Vocabulary, 31–32
Voting, by students, 21, 25–26, 29

W

We're in This Together (picture prompt), 120–121
"What You Are Doing" cards, 76
"What's Happening?"
    activity, 71–72
    cards, 74
What's in the Box? (picture prompt), 118–119
What's So Funny? (picture prompt), 126–127
Writer of the week activity, 42
Writing
    importance of, 2
    as puzzle pieces, 27–28
    student samples, 11
    See also Written responses; *specific prompt types*
Writing Assessment Information Fact Sheet, 12
Writing relay, 43
Written responses
    coding, 36, 37
    scribing class responses, 23–26
    self-editing, 26
    story components, 23–26, 29–35
    title, choosing, 25–26, 35
    See also specific prompt types

About the Authors

Hope Sara Blecher-Sass, Ed.D., is the supervisor of language arts, social studies, and media for North Plainfield Public School District in New Jersey. She has been a literacy coach and an educator for twenty-four years, teaching special education, English as a second language, and English language arts. She lives in Clark, New Jersey, with her family.

Maryellen Moffitt has been an educator for twenty-eight years, teaching fifth and sixth graders and gifted and talented students. She coordinates the gifted and talented program of Roselle Public School District in New Jersey. She lives in Rahway, New Jersey.

Interested in a *See It, Be It, Write It* workshop?

Hope and Maryellen provide on-site professional development for administrators, staff, students, and parents. Go to www.hope4education.com for more information.

Teachers, Administrators, Librarians, Counselors, Youth Workers, and Social Workers
Help us create the resources you need to support the kids you serve.

Join the Free Spirit Advisory Board

In order to make our books and other products even more beneficial for children and teens, the Free Spirit Advisory Board provides valuable feedback on content, art, title concepts, and more. You can help us identify what educators need to help kids think for themselves, succeed in school and life, and make a difference in the world. Apply today! For more information, go to **www.freespirit.com/educators.**

More Great Books from Free Spirit

Differentiating Instruction in the Regular Classroom
How to Reach and Teach All Learners, Grades 3–12
by Diane Heacox, Ed.D.

*176 pp., softcover, 8½" x 11".
Grades 3–12. Macintosh and
Windows compatible CD-ROM.*

Making Differentiation a Habit
How to Ensure Success in Academically Diverse Classrooms
by Diane Heacox, Ed.D.

*198 pp., softcover, 8½" x 11".
Grades K–12. Macintosh and
Windows compatible CD-ROM.*

Teaching Beyond the Test
Differentiated Project-Based Learning in a Standards-Based Age, Grades 6 & Up
*by Phil Schlemmer, M.Ed.,
and Dori Schlemmer*

*256 pp., softcover, 8½" x 11".
Grades K–6. Macintosh and
Windows compatible CD-ROM.*

Projects & Presentations for K–6 Students
Preparing Kids to Be Confident, Effective Communicators
*by Phil Schlemmer, M.Ed.,
and Dori Schlemmer*

*240 pp., softcover, 8½" x 11".
Grades K–6. Macintosh and
Windows compatible CD-ROM.*

RTI Success
Proven Tools and Strategies for Schools and Classrooms
*by Elizabeth Whitten, Ph.D.,
Kelli J. Esteves, Ed.D.,
and Alice Woodrow, Ed.D.*

*256 pp., softcover, 8½" x 11".
Grades K–6. Macintosh and
Windows compatible CD-ROM.*

Quick and Lively Classroom Activities
Meaningful Ways to Keep Kids Engaged During Transition Time, Downtime, or Anytime
*by Linda Nason McElherne, M.A.,
illustrated by Ken Vinton, M.A.*

*184 pp., softcover, illust., 8½" x 11".
Grades 3–6. Macintosh and
Windows compatible CD-ROM.*

free spirit
PUBLISHING®

**Meeting kids' social,
emotional & educational
needs since 1983**

For pricing information, to place an order, or to request a free catalog, contact:

**217 Fifth Avenue North • Suite 200 • Minneapolis, MN 55401-1299
toll-free 800.735.7323 • local 612.338.2068 • fax 612.337.5050
help4kids@freespirit.com • www.freespirit.com**